Democracy in the Digital Age
How we'll vote and what we'll vote about

Costa Vayenas lives in Switzerland, where ordinary citizens are called upon to be legislators. He has voted in over 200 legislative proposals at all three levels of government: local, cantonal and federal. The insights he gained from this process have been useful in his professional life as an investment analyst. Asset prices, after all, are also a function of how well a country is governed. He is the editor of an 800-page book on the emerging markets (Bloomsbury). He was Head of Research for the emerging markets at UBS, and has worked as an analyst in London, New York and Zurich. One of his reports was cited in *The Financial Times* as having triggered a currency crisis. Another featured on the front page of *The Wall Street Journal* under "What's News". He has lectured at the University of Zurich and has been a guest lecturer at the Swiss Federal Institute of Technology. It was an invitation to speak at the latter's Institute of Science, Technology and Policy that was the trigger for this book, which describes how democracy is being disrupted by digitalization and the profound consequences of that disruption.

Democracy in the Digital Age

How we'll vote and what we'll vote about

Costa Vayenas

Arena Books

First published in 2017 by Arena Books
Arena Books
6 Southgate Green
Bury St. Edmunds
IP33 2BL

www.arenabooks.co.uk
Distributed in America by Ingram International, One Ingram Blvd.,
PO Box 3006, La Vergne, TN 37086-1985, USA.

Costa Vayenas
Democracy in the Digital Age *How we'll vote and what we'll vote about*

British Library cataloguing in Publication Data. A Catalogue record of this
book is available from the British Library.

ISBN-13   978-1-909421-99-8

BIC classifications:- LNDS, LND, JFCX, JFH, JHBA, HBA.

Printed and bound by Lightning Source UK

Cover design
by Jason Anscomb

Typeset in
Times New Roman

TABLE OF CONTENTS

EXHIBITS

PREFACE AND ACKNOWLEDGEMENTS

The idea for this book originated from research I had done about the impact that digital technology can have in opening up new markets. It struck me that while digitalization was changing all aspects of how modern societies operate, there was one sector that appeared to have been left untouched.

Disintermediation, short for "cutting out the intermediary or middle man between two parties", was happening everywhere, except in arguably the most important arena of all – democracy. Was there a special reason, I wondered, why the job of the lawmaker had not changed in the digital age? How long would the grand buildings housing parliaments still have activity on their floors, while the grand buildings housing stock exchanges had already gone quiet?

Looking for answers, I found evidence that disintermediation is under way in politics too – globally. I wrote this book to highlight the evidence and consider the implications of this coming disruption.

For enriching my project, I would like to thank Thomas Bernauer, Ken Corroon, Phil Gramm, Peter Kurer, Richard Ligon, Dieter Ruloff, Uwe Serdült, Markus Spillmann, and last but not least, Barbara, Celine and Alix.

FOREWORD

By Thomas Bernauer, Professor of Political Science and Head of the Institute of Science, Technology and Policy at the Swiss Federal Institute of Technology

In a definition commonly attributed to Abraham Lincoln, democracy means government of the people, by the people, and for the people. No government in the world is perfect in this regard, but some are better than others. Autocrats typically claim that their policies are what people want, though without free and fair elections or free news media and civil liberties it is impossible to say, and most often entirely implausible that this is true. Even in mature democracies, parochial interest groups oftentimes shape policies in ways that cater to their interests, rather than to the welfare of the country's population.

The advent of the digital age raises hopes that ever lower costs and higher speeds of information flows over electronic networks will facilitate interaction between policymakers and citizens. What this will do to the quality of democracy, in the sense defined above, remains contested. Optimists believe that the digital age will also bring digital democracy (what exactly this means remains open to debate), and this in turn will create more transparency of, and greater accountability by, policymakers for citizens. As a result, policies are likely to align better with what the majority of citizens want. Pessimists point out that faster and cheaper communication could lead to more volatile and poorly thought-through policy choices, relative to the traditional decision process where representatives meet in person, are able to familiarize themselves with substantive policy issues, debate, and strike compromises. Hence they fear that digital democracy harbours the risk of an unstable and conflict-prone tyranny by the majority.

Costa Vayenas seeks to navigate between these two extremes, pointing out the benefits of digitalizing the democratic decision process, but also the challenges or risks. He also points to many open questions, for instance whether this could reverse the trend of declining political participation by younger citizens, or how digital democracy could work in very large countries, for instance India. The example of Switzerland, which is discussed in depth and receives much praise, actually highlights two issues. First, Switzerland has been very reluctant to digitalize direct democracy (initiatives, referendums), both in terms of collecting signatures and voting on proposals. Most citizens and policy observers fear that making the system faster and cheaper to operate may increase voter fatigue and result in more extreme (usually right- or left-wing populist-type) policies. Second, strong checks and balances and subsidiarity in the system have developed over a long period of time. These have made the decision process very slow, but by-and-large have worked well in protecting minorities, dealing with differences in a country that has four languages and several religions, and have helped make the country politically stable and wealthy. This suggests that digital democracy is not a panacea for achieving transparent, accountable, and welfare-enhancing governance in countries around the world. Rather, it is one additional tool in the broader repertoire of decision-making mechanisms that can be very useful, provided the institutions in which it is embedded make sure it works to the advantage of citizens and protects minorities.

INTRODUCTION

The three-century-old ritual, by which the people need to queue up at the polling station every few years to assign a multi-year blank check to representatives to make the law, is a model that was designed when mail delivery was new and unreliable.

Unlike the disruption caused by digitalization in postal services, where people were happy with the product – mail – but just switched to another form of delivery – email – the people worldwide seem less and less impressed with the product that their representatives have been delivering.

Technology now offers the people, who in democracies have the say about the political system, the opportunity, for better or worse, to exercise greater control. Whereas senders and receivers of mail probably did not think they needed digital post on the device they used for making calls, they happily used it when available. With representative government it is the other way round: the data shows that the people desperately want better outcomes, and now technology is giving them new possibilities to try and achieve that.

Technology is now making it possible for the people to petition their government electronically, for the people to launch initiatives online, to vote online and, most radically, to compete with their legislature or even to replace it. Technology can now directly connect the people to the server where legislation is being prepared on their behalf. Technology holds the capacity to transfer power directly to the people.

This book was written to address the profound change that modern technology has the capacity to make in democracy itself. The idea that everything can be disintermediated in the internet age, except the job of the middle men in politics does not seem plausible. That no further shifts in power to the people can occur is also not supported by history. Constitutions fix a system in place, but every national constitution also provides the means to change the system. What we know from history is that the question of who can vote about what using which means is never settled.

Had the representative model been invented today, it would almost certainly have been configured differently. Just as the evolution occurred on the question of *who* could vote, it seems inevitable that in the digital age the question will now turn to *how* people vote and *what* they vote on. These changes may work to improve the quality of government or make it worse, but these changes appear to be the inevitable evolution to the next iteration of how free people want to organize themselves politically.

CHAPTER 1

A TECHNOLOGICAL CHALLENGE TO THE FOUNDING FATHERS

Very little has changed in the machinery of representative democracy since the late 1700s. As in those early days, in most countries the people still have to wait for years at a time for the privilege of queuing up at the ballot box. Between those visits, policy decisions that can have momentous consequences continue to lie outside of the people's remit.

This bargain is starting to unravel. The technology by which the people receive their information and make their will known is being revolutionized.

That technology influences how the people instruct their representatives, is as old as recorded history. Over thousands of years, the ballot has been many different things: a show of hands, the spoken word, light and dark pebbles, engravings on bits of clay, entries on small wax tablets, olive leaves, pieces of bronze, papyrus, parchment, vellum, marbles, the lifting of swords, and paper.[1] Since the beginning of the twenty-first century, in more and more places, the ballot has become a series of electronic digits transmitted far from the traditional polling booth. In recent years, hundreds of government-sponsored and government-supervised elections over the internet have taken place in many countries, including in Australia, Canada, Estonia, France, India, Mexico, the Netherlands, New Zealand, Norway, Portugal, Switzerland, the United Kingdom and the United States.[2] The evolution of the ballot is continuing, therefore.

Estonia, the country where the software for Skype was developed, moved beyond the experimental phase of electronic voting by introducing legally-binding voting via the internet in 2005. The entire Estonian electorate no longer needs to go to the polls – they can vote from anywhere in the world.

What are we to call this new kind of ballot? A digital ballot? An electronic ballot? An internet ballot? Here it is abbreviated as the *i-ballot*.

A ballot can reinforce the pursuit of happiness or undermine it, but a ballot can never be neutral. That being the case, the ease with which people can get access to a ballot matters. When technology changes profoundly, the effects can be spectacular. When technology permitted us to add the "e" to mail, we sent and received far more mail than before. If we now add the "i" to ballot, what are we going to get more of? Might we get a higher turnout of voters? More elections? Might we be asked to vote about new kinds of things?

Slowly but surely we are getting a growing body of data, experience and academic research on this topic, which offers some first answers to these questions. The data from Estonia, France and Switzerland provides the longest time series in this area, allowing for some meaningful initial comparisons.

The key takeaway from the Estonian data is that the i-ballot there has resulted in a higher voter turnout overall.[3] These results confirm what one might have expected intuitively, namely, that if something is easier to do, like voting from home in your pyjamas, then more people are likely to try it, but only if they think what they're doing is relevant. That last requirement – only if it is worth doing – is a condition that still needs to be fulfilled in the digital age in order to get out the vote.

Let's look at the data. Even before the Estonian case, we already had empirical evidence that when the state makes it a bit easier for citizens to vote, then more people are likely to vote. This evidence comes from the world's only postal democracy, Switzerland. In that country every eligible citizen, regardless of where they are registered in the world, automatically receives a ballot in the post, complete with a self-addressed return envelope, whether they want it or not. A long-term study that looked at the impact on voter turnout following the introduction of postal voting in Switzerland found that it resulted in an increased voter turnout of around four percentage points.[4] At first glance, that is a surprisingly low number considering that the ballot arrives at your home without you requesting it, and includes a return envelope addressed to the ballot-counting authority. How much easier can it be than that? But that is also a reminder of how uninterested the average person is in politics – they don't even want to open the envelope. Getting people to vote is hard work. On the other hand, a permanent increase of four percentage points in voter turnout shows that more convenience *does* make a difference. And given how narrow some election wins are, four percentage points can make a huge difference in some places. Seen from that perspective, a permanent increase of four percentage points is a big deal in politics.

If four extra percentage points are what happens in a postal democracy where the postal system works well, what would happen in a digital democracy? It would be reasonable to assume that pushing a button on one's smart phone should be even easier than posting a letter, thereby increasing voter turnout by more than in a postal democracy. And this is also what the current evidence shows: the i-ballot has increased voter turnout in Estonia by around six percentage points. That's an even bigger deal in politics.

Again, at first glance, it may be surprising that this new technology has not resulted in even higher voter turnouts. But here we have to overcome the first rule of getting out the vote: What's in it for me? Why should I bother to vote? Data comparing internet voting in France and Switzerland underlines this.

In France in 2012, French citizens living abroad were, for the first time, able to vote for their own members of the lower house of the legislature. The i-ballot was one of the options available.[5] Testing started in 2003 for selected elections for French residents living abroad, but the i-ballot was not offered for presidential elections, referendums or elections to the European parliament.[6] For those elections, French citizens living abroad still need to find a car, bus, train, boat or plane to take them to the local consulate or embassy. After more than a decade of experience with this limited i-ballot, the data shows that the French living abroad are twice as likely to make the effort to get to a polling booth to vote in an election that they believe matters, like the election of the president, rather than using the internet to vote from home in an election that they feel is less important.[7] The main insight here is that it is not the type of ballot – papyrus, small pebbles or the i-ballot – that determines voter turnout, but the importance of the issue being decided. Even if it is possible to vote over the internet, therefore, few will waste their time pushing the send button for issues they think are unimportant.

In contrast to the French, the Swiss approach during the current test phase permits the i-ballot for all votes, including for the really important ones. The result is that five times as many Swiss expatriates use the i-ballot compared to French expatriates.[8] The Swiss data reinforces the intuitive view that more voters would opt for the i-ballot if it were available to vote on things that matter to them.[9]

The key inference, therefore, is that the new technology can result in a higher turnout *if* the election in question is relevant to voters. This is also confirmed by the data about one of the great mysteries of voter-turnout: Will the i-ballot cause more young people to vote? A report published by the British parliament's Commission on Digital Democracy, set up by the Speaker of the House of Commons, John Bercow, was of the view that "there is a substantial appetite for online voting in the UK, particularly among young people".[10] The report, published in 2015, set the ambition that "by 2020 secure online voting should be an option for all voters."[11]

But the data from Estonia reveal that the i-ballot has *not* resulted in an increase in the share of voters in the 18-24 age group. Throughout the world, when voting is not compulsory, the overwhelming majority of the 18-24 age group is not easily persuaded to go and vote. A review of many academic studies up until 2015 on what kinds of people vote by internet found that the 18-24 age group continued to be uninterested.[12] They are not going to be cajoled by parents or politicians to download apps that don't interest them. Strategists targeting the 18-24 age group will need to find other ways to connect with these young people.

As more experience is gathered on holding binding elections over the internet in developed countries, the topic is beginning to attract more attention in more countries. A 2016 survey of academic papers on the i-ballot by the University of New South Wales in Canberra, Australia, found an increased output in academic research on this topic in the following developing countries (ranked according to the number of academic papers): Nigeria, Brazil, Indonesia, Argentina, India, Iran, Jordan, South Africa, Colombia, Pakistan, Tanzania, Ghana, Ecuador, Lebanon, Mauritius, Mexico, Thailand, Turkey and Uganda.[13]

The United States is the country one might have expected to see take the lead in introducing the i-ballot, but so far the picture has been a mixed patchwork, reflecting the competing centres of power in that federal republic. Currently thirty-one US states offer the i-ballot to military and overseas voters. The lack of experimentation for US residents appears uncharacteristically hesitant for a country that is home to Silicon Valley.[14] One reason for this hesitance is that, everywhere, everyone appears to be facing the same worrying questions about the i-ballot. Is it safe? This is a wonderful time for the lawyers. Already there is a build-up of case law on this technology in many countries, including in Argentina, Australia, Brazil, Estonia, France, Finland, Germany, India, Mexico, Switzerland, the United States and Venezuela.[15]

Some voters keep suing on the basis that this new technology is undermining their rights. The legal challenges come from three main angles: first, that the technology might not ensure the *secrecy* of each individual's choice (like when you mark your cross on a piece of paper privately behind a curtain at a polling booth), second, that what happens on the inside of the computer is not *verifiable* by ordinary members of the public (like when election observers can see how the ballot boxes are emptied onto counting tables to be counted and the people doing the counting can be monitored), and third, that each vote might not be given *equal* treatment if different types of ballots and different mechanisms are used for recording, transmitting, sorting, counting and storing votes in different constituencies. This latter point becomes especially important in very tight races and when recounts are needed and a tiny number of votes can make the difference. It is then that the curtain gets pulled away to reveal the hidden world of voting technology. In the US, we learnt about the "hanging chads" affecting some of the ballots in the Bush vs. Gore election. In Switzerland, when the curtain was pulled away after one particularly close election, it revealed the surprising information that some jurisdictions did not actually count the paper ballots, they just weighed them![16] Strange things have happened, therefore, with the tallying of paper ballots. In the digital era, it thus needs to be transparent what happens to the i-ballots on their way to an electronic database.

The big concern, of course, is that computers can be hacked, that it might be possible to see who voted for whom, and that the election results could be manipulated. Despite these concerns, the continued efforts to roll out the i-ballot in many countries show three main influences at work. The first is that technology is constantly evolving to address these worries. The second is that, in some countries, citizens' trust in their authorities is very high, which means they don't believe that their independent election agency would run elections using unsafe voting systems. And third, the public has gotten used to doing all kinds of important things via the internet – voting seems to be one more of these things that is inevitably shifting from paper to the internet.

Where the potential for damage is much bigger with the i-ballot than for a purely paper-based system is in the order of magnitude: When things go wrong with a centralized computer-based system, the errors might not become apparent or they could become spectacularly so, in that everyone's "secret" vote gets posted on the internet, say. This latter type of accident almost happened when there was a near-miss with half the i-ballots in Norway in 2013 as a result of an error in the encryption code.[17] If this type of thing can happen in Norway, a wealthy country with a technocratic administration, then we might well ask what could all go wrong if the i-ballot were to be launched in less well-prepared countries that have fewer resources and lower standards of transparency and governance?

Given what has already been stolen from government databases, we can probably not be confident that the "secret" electronic ballots of an entire electorate won't one day appear on the web. In April 2016, it became known that the entire Mexican electoral roll, containing the names and addresses of over ninety million Mexicans, appeared on a cloud server, unencrypted. It was found by a member of the public. Also in that month, the personal information of around seventy million people from the Philippines' voters' roll appears to have been compromised, and the data of fifty million Turkish citizens was posted online. Attempts to hack polling systems in the 2016 US presidential election were widely reported, but no case showing an erroneous vote tally as a result of the hacking probes was proven in any US court.[18]

Bad as these headlines have been, they have not yet heralded the end of the computer age. On the contrary, what each of these cases does is to push the victims up the learning curve, just like in all other spheres of life. We have to go back to one of Aesop's fables, about a cat, pretending to be a sack as it lies in wait for some chickens, to be reminded that we learn from experience. In Aesop's fable, the rooster warns the chickens that he'd seen many sacks before, but never one that had the teeth of a live cat. That bit of advice saved the chickens on that day. The cat had to invent new tricks to try and catch them on another day.

Over time, it will get harder and harder for the bad guys to try and hack the most secure IT systems using the same old tricks. Of course, they will keep looking for new ways to achieve their target. But those who want to learn from experience are upping their game in terms of both improved governance and improved technology to make for a more secure i-ballot. It is clear that this will require a much higher standard than used by e-banking because it would need to address all of the known security weaknesses, including the assumption that everyone's home computer and mobile phone are unsafe and that the postal system is unsafe, which means that no verification codes can be sent via these routes. On-going theoretical and practical work is being done to make electronic voting systems safer.[19] Part of the solution might include an additional layer of security in that each eligible voter receives a relatively tamper-proof chip – like the biometric chip in passports – that can be read by a device to help authenticate the voter. The IT landscape is changing daily. We cannot reasonably say what kind of IT software and hardware solutions may be available in the years ahead, but the working assumption is that the good guys will be able to fight back with increasing degrees of sophistication. Long before governments are able to protect their databases and networks with the next big thing, quantum-resistant cryptography, the playing field may start to tilt in favour of the more advanced states being able to run more secure online elections.

The one area where no degree of encryption will help to protect the integrity of an election process is in the area identified more than two thousand years ago by the Roman statesman Cicero: "A nation can survive its fools, and even the ambitious. But it cannot survive treason from within." Therefore, just as importantly as having the best IT solutions, countries that want to run honest elections over the internet will need to have a superior governance framework in place, with many checks and balances. The significance of this governance dimension appears to be wholly underappreciated in many places.[20] A review of the near-miss in Norway, described earlier, also pointed to governance issues – the process was too rushed to do all the checks.[21]

We have to assume, therefore, that we are going to learn about a case, or perhaps even several cases, in which an electronic election is proven *in court* to have not been "free and fair" because of tampering. Bad as that would be as a headline, it is unlikely to result in the collapse of a democracy or the end of the use of computers for voting purposes. We have the case of the 2016 presidential election in Austria in which a court invalidated the election result and required the election to be re-held. What the Austrian case showed was that the rule of law worked, the election was annulled and re-run, the country moved on and now everyone knows that a presidential election in Austria that is not correctly run will be annulled and rerun as many times as required to get it right. In that sense, the episode served to reinforce the people's faith in their institutions. But that won't be the case everywhere, of course.

The distrust in the ability of the authorities to run free and fair elections in the United States appears higher than in Austria. There are several cases in US history where it is still disputed whether the right candidate won – and that was just using a paper-based system.[22] Even today, the legend continues that the 1960 US presidential election may have been rigged and the wrong person won.[23]

The apparent scepticism by large enough numbers of US voters about the authorities' ability to ensure honest elections was an issue given prominence by Donald Trump during the 2016 presidential campaign.[24] And within days of taking office, he tweeted that a "major investigation" into voter fraud would take place. There was talk that perhaps three to five million people had voted illegally. [25] These suspicions will feed into the speed with which the US adopts the i-ballot. The idea that millions of illegal people might be able to vote from mobile devices for the opposition should be sufficiently dystopian to keep this new technology far away from many US electoral districts.

Elsewhere, where trust in the authorities is higher, and the focus is on the security of the voting technology itself, the relentless drive by software and hardware developers to earn their living by enhancing security, will support those forces looking to roll out a more secure i-ballot in more places.

The evidence so far is that the journey towards the rollout of the i-ballot has already begun. We are heading for a tipping point, to an era where unprecedented numbers of people will use an electronic voting device, from anywhere in the world, to choose and instruct their representatives – something that has never happened before.

The question is where does this lead to? The easy part is that it leads away from queues at polling stations. That's the logistical part. But it is highly likely that this technological innovation will be about a lot more than queues at polling stations. The i-ballot is, over time, likely to result in a fundamental shift in the balance of power back to the people. If the polling booth is now an app on your handheld device, it could lead to higher voter turnouts under certain conditions. More voters from a particular group could shift the outcome of an election – either they will reinforce a trend or they will help to erode it. If a few more younger voters vote on occasion, they'll erode some of the voting power of the older voters, who vote more often. If more minority voters and more voters from abroad vote, they may have more nuanced views than the mainstream. In very close races, these additional voters could have even more power. Since a state-of-the-art technology would mean that spoilt ballots are impossible – every vote is correctly recorded – the i-ballot could change the outcome of very close votes. In the 2000 US presidential race, it took thirty-five days to learn that George Bush beat Al Gore by 537 votes out of nearly six million in Florida, where the presidential election was decided. However, there were 175,010 *rejected* ballots, 113,820 of which had votes for two or more candidates and

61,190 for no presidential candidate.[26] A secure electronic voting system might have produced different numbers, and perhaps even a different outcome.

The i-ballot is the twenty-first century equivalent of a major upgrade of democracy. It will become cheaper and easier to formally obtain the people's consent. The "transaction costs", to use the academic jargon, will fall dramatically – both for the voter and for the state. The implications of this efficiency gain will differ from country to country. Consider the example of India, the world's largest democracy, where the most recent general election took six weeks from the start of voting until the results were announced. It is no surprise, therefore, that experimentation with the i-ballot has started in this large producer of information technology. The first binding internet voting in India took place in municipal elections in 2011 in Gandhinagar, in the state of Gujarat.[27] According to the local election commission, the switch "will help citizens who have access to the internet, cast their votes online, without standing in long queues, which are a deterrent."[28] Here, as in all other cases so far, the reason for the service being offered is as a *convenience* to the clients, the people. But its real disruptive potential lies elsewhere: It opens the possibility, unforeseen by the founding fathers of old constitutions, that it would become logistically much easier to consult the people on more things more frequently. Once that realization dawns in more places, someone, somewhere is going to become the first to want to try out such a disruptive thought. If the ballot is a button on your mobile phone, should the app only be used for general elections every few years? What about the in-between years? Should the people not be consulted more often on more things? If not, why not?

To argue that this new voting technology, once it has been shown to be sufficiently secure, should never be used, or only be used sparingly, every few years, say, will be like arguing that the internet should only be used sparingly to protect the job of the middle man, which otherwise would be disintermediated away. The argument that the role of the legislative representative – a job profile – requires special protection in the digital age from the internet's ability to eliminate it, is an argument that has technology and political trends stacked against it.

The growing availability and use of technology enabling electronic voting will, over time, open up a Pandora's box. It will challenge the centuries-old customs of a representative system that was built in the days when the majority of the voters were labouring in the fields and knew very little about the policy debates taking place in a faraway legislature.

The availability of new technology by which the people can choose to make their will known, combined with the growing complexity faced by modern-day legislatures, is hastening the decline of the representative system as we've known it.

CHAPTER 2

TECHNOLOGY AND NEW FREEDOMS

Where technology leads, society and the law eventually follow. The switch to binding elections via remote electronic devices is now well underway in dozens of countries. For the first time in history, technology is making it possible for the most connected citizenry ever to be consulted more easily on more things.

Technology can make it easier to exercise an existing right, like voting, but from home, say, instead of having to queue up outside a polling station. Technology can also be a very powerful force for the creation of new political rights. This dimension of technology is so intrinsic that it is often overlooked, but it can have profound implications. When the first amendment to the US Constitution guaranteed freedom "of the press" in 1791 – that right could not have been granted had Gutenberg not invented a new technology, the printing press. First came the printing press, then society got used to its advantages, and then came the law enshrining it as a fundamental right.

A similar thing is happening with the internet. First it was an exciting new toy, then society came to see it as indispensable – a survey showed that a large majority of adults across the world regard the internet as a "fundamental right"[29] – and then court rulings and laws started saying the same. By 2016, the human rights dimension of the internet had even reached the global rule-setting stage when the United Nations' Human Rights Council drew up a resolution on the "promotion, protection and enjoyment of human rights on the Internet".[30] Again, this shows the usual sequencing: First comes the new technology, then society's response to it, and then the law catches up by validating the prevailing view. And when the law has been written and modern-day courts in liberal democracies are asked to interpret it further, then the courts tend to err on the side of chipping away at the might of the state and awarding even greater personal freedoms and rights to the little man.

That has been the tendency since at least the late 1700s, and there is no indication that this will be any different in the twenty-first century. Rather, it appears likely that new technology is going to speed up the creation of new political rights in our century. Sometimes this can lead to strange developments that would have been incomprehensible in a time before the new technology was known. For example, in 2014, the European Union's highest court ruled that there was a "right to be forgotten".[31] This means that a resident in the EU has the right to force an internet search engine to delink that individual's name from searches that violate that individual's right to privacy.

An example of how new technology can facilitate the exercise of existing rights, thereby placing more power in citizens' hands, comes to us from the Netherlands, where new technology has made it easier to collect signatures for a popular initiative. The 2014 law permitted the use of "electronic means", but did not specify how, precisely, this should be done.[32] This opening allowed someone to develop an app that made it possible for supporters of an initiative to sign it by using a finger on a mobile phone screen.[33]

New technology is rarely a neutral thing, therefore; it is a disrupter. Similarly, technology has the potential to influence the most fundamental feature of democracy – the outcome of elections. One way to illustrate this is to look at the impact on election outcomes brought about by a change in something as basic as the technology used for the ballot. There was a time when elections were not conducted by secret ballot, neither in ancient Greece or Rome, nor in the United Kingdom or in the United States. In the UK, the secret ballot was only introduced as late as 1872,[34] and later in the US. Before the introduction of secret ballots, one method of voting was for voters to verbally tell an appointed election official at the polling station who their vote was for. The official then had to record that and tally the results. When society decided it was time to switch to a secret ballot, a different voting technology was required. The new method delivered its objective – a secret ballot – but it also changed election outcomes. In one study, voter turnout in the US *declined* by around seven percentage points after the introduction of the secret ballot.[35] A possible explanation for this decline is that some voters had only gone to the polls as a result of pressure from their landlord or their employer, or as a result of gifts from a particular candidate. The introduction of the secret ballot also discriminated against those who could not read or write, thus keeping them away from the polls.

Another effect of the introduction of the secret ballot, noted after Rome introduced it in 139 BC, was that gifts from candidates were now redistributed to specific tribes or regions. Sometimes the gifts were provided *after* the regional result became available, thereby confirming the quid pro quo.[36] The same principle exists today. Voters will support the candidates whose policies they believe will benefit them personally (or their family, tribe or region). An analysis of internet votes cast in Estonia (based on, inter alia, the IP address of the computer used, the number of times voting occurred from that computer, the time-interval between each vote from that computer, and the time of the day the vote took place), has led to the conclusion that some family members tend to vote together, implying that voting preferences within families are not a big secret. There is also evidence that some households have eager beavers who vote on behalf of those family members who are too lazy, disinterested or busy to vote themselves.[37] The secrecy of the ballot was and remains a relative concept, therefore. It appears that society only cares if the violation of the secrecy is non-consensual.

Given, as we have just seen, that technology can impact election turnouts and, therefore, outcomes, we should expect voters to favour the introduction of new voting technology if they believe it will deliver a better outcome for them. Even if the arguments for and against the i-ballot are publicly fought around other topics, like cybersecurity, secrecy of the ballot, modernity and convenience or about noble principles of upgrading democracy, ultimately this is a fight about something very different; this is about who will have more political power in the digital era. This is about who will gain by going electronic and who will lose.

The evidence since around 2005 is that, in just a short space of time, new voting technology has created important new freedoms: eligible citizens have acquired new freedoms in terms of *when* they can vote (anytime, day or night, from the time early votes are accepted) and *where* they can vote (from anywhere). This technology has even created the new freedom (which exists in Estonia) for voters *to change their vote*, as often as they wish, switching it from one candidate to another, until the polls close. The reasons for such a feature are two-fold: first, because the technology makes it possible (that's what technological innovation is all about, after all – if the app offers the feature, some will use it), and second, because it makes it less likely for coercion to occur at home or at work since voters can keep changing their preferences from anywhere at any time. All three of these new freedoms were triggered by a new voting technology – a paper-based system would not make it easy to keep a polling booth open 24/7 or allow voters to change their vote after they had cast it or allowed voters to vote from anywhere.

While the above-mentioned new freedoms fall under the category of *how* people vote, the new technology has not yet triggered big shifts in terms of *what* voters can vote about. But that will likely be next. Since neither technology nor cost will be a restriction on how often people can vote or about what they can vote, we are likely to see a shift to more voting about *issues*, as opposed to mere elections for candidates or parties. Over time, this could lead to the type of voting arrangement we see at a company shareholder meeting. In its most basic form, a shareholder receives a letter from the board setting out the issues to be voted on at the upcoming annual general meeting. The shareholder can then choose to be personally involved and vote on each and every issue, or the shareholder could decide to choose to ask a proxy to take care of these decisions.

It is perfectly feasible that an electronic voting platform could be built to replicate this shareholder meeting arrangement to allow an eligible, authenticated voter to transfer voting rights to a proxy. Since we're in the digital era, such an electronic platform could offer even fancier options. Who should that proxy be? Should it be a member of the legislature or could it be any eligible citizen? Once authenticated and logged into the official voter platform, a voter could search for a delegate from the voter's role. If we choose our representative by issue, then our chosen delegate or delegates only have the votes to represent us on specific issues. If we choose our representative as our "trustee", as Edmund Burke (1729-1797) advocated, then it is exactly the same as voting for a member of parliament under the old system to represent us on "all things" until the next general election. The Edmund Burke option is for people who do not want to be bothered with even more political choices.

Conceptually, such an electronic platform is not rocket science – it is not unlike buying a product online or making a banking payment. When we select our product, we make a payment, i.e. we allocate our "vote" (units of cash or points) to someone. Allocating a proxy vote by issue constitutes the same principle. Each voter on the voter's roll has one vote for each and every piece of legislation that needs to be voted on. Very rarely we may want to vote ourselves directly. At other times, we're fine to allocate our vote to our delegate or delegates. But in a democracy in the digital age, technology allows us to have that choice.

Up to now we have merely scratched the surface of some of the features that an electronic voting platform could offer in terms of the mechanics of voting. In a shareholder's meeting, how do the issues get listed in that letter to shareholders? There has to be some pre-process. We could build a pre-process into our electronic voting platform. We could contribute our own ideas on petitions and initiatives that could be voted on. Technology is not a restriction here either.

We could take it even further: In the same way that people write online reviews about products and services that they feel they have something to say about, in a democracy that enfranchises its citizens with new digital tools, eligible citizens could log onto the platform where legislation is being drafted to comment on the text. Digital technology will facilitate the submission of suggestions for amendments to draft legislation and allow eligible voters to endorse or reject those proposals. Depending on how the constitution is modified to deal with these technological options, proposals for amendments (or even fully-fledged initiatives) could either become a petition for parliament to consider (i.e. parliament would still retain a high degree of control over the final wording of the law) or citizens would be empowered to permit citizen-approved texts to become binding legislation (i.e. parliament would have no power to stop what the people have just decided). The dial can be turned quite a bit between these two extremes.

At this point, if not already much earlier, you might have started to become concerned about all the choices that voters might face and what this might mean in terms of the time that would be required to participate in such a process, and you might have thought about the ability, interest and willingness of ordinary voters to involve themselves in such a level of detail. But that is what has been happening in all other areas that are connected to the internet. That is what disintermediation in the digital age is doing. We're even supposed to be managing our own money directly via fintech platforms now. Compared to that, the political choices are easy. The idea that everything can be communicated by citizens via a mobile app, except the holy grail of what our representatives in parliament should be doing on our behalf, is the odd idea in the digital age.

Other than clicking on the Edmund Burke tab on the electronic platform, another way to deal with the risk of an information overload due to too many proposals for amendments or new initiatives is simply to raise the bar: for any initiative to be considered, it needs to be endorsed by a large number of eligible voters. The Germans appear prepared for this, whereas the British do not yet appear to have appreciated the potential consequences, in the digital era, of asking their citizens to ping the authorities with their legislative demands. In several German states (the Länder), reforms in the 1990s started making it easier for more places to permit citizens to launch popular initiatives. These typically require the support of at least twenty-five per cent of voters for legislation and fifty per cent for constitutional amendments. In contrast, in the UK, just one hundred thousand signatures are required for the UK parliament's petition portal, representing just 0.2 per cent of the UK's voting-age population. This low hurdle in the UK is evidence that this portal does not (yet) represent real people's power – the petitions can safely be ignored when inconvenient. But it does appear that this low threshold in the UK has underestimated the extent to which the digital age is empowering citizens. The day may come when an inconvenient petition goes viral and becomes a little more difficult to ignore. These online petitions are prototype digital legislatures. The media are full of stories from all over the world of how ordinary citizens are launching online petitions that are resulting in new legislation. Cases range from making it illegal for women to be required to wear high heels at work (UK) and new laws against stalking (Germany).

Technology's capacity to create new political rights in the twenty-first century should not be underestimated. How this progresses, and the pace at which it develops, depends on several variables and the paths that will be selected.

Each country is unique. Each country will, therefore, have its own distinctive triggers that determine the pace at which change happens. But everywhere, the outcome will be influenced by the interplay between the forces for and against giving the people more of a say on more things. These forces have both domestic and global drivers that reinforce each other. An idea whose time has come can quickly spill over from one country to another. When it became trendy to introduce the secret ballot in the late 1800s in the UK and the US, that new arrangement was referred to as "the Australian ballot", because that's where it had first been introduced in the modern era. An idea about how to improve democracy in Australia spilled over to the UK and the US.

If citizens in more and more democracies start giving themselves the right to decide more things more often with the use of new technology, it will eventually have an impact on the discourse everywhere. We can visualize what this experimentation might look like using a matrix that shows the interplay between shifts in how we will vote in the future and what we will be voting on.

As shown in Exhibit 1, the assumption is that different societies are going to approach these new possibilities in different ways. The vertical line defines how we vote (by paper or electronically by i-ballot, say). At the bottom end of that line we have zero innovation, that is to say, no internet voting exists. That's the status quo in most of the world.

As countries move away from the current paper-based system towards electronic voting options, they move up that *how* line, ranking more highly in terms of electronic innovation and electronic convenience for voters.

EXHIBIT 1: VISUALIZING THE DIMENSIONS OF HOW WE WILL VOTE AND WHAT WE WILL VOTE ABOUT IN THE DIGITAL AGE

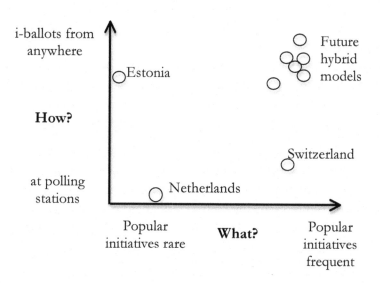

The evidence suggests that there are shifts taking place along both axes: there is a drift both up the *how* line and sideways on the *what* line. We should expect to see a dynamic picture for the matrix in Exhibit 1. Switzerland, for example, plans to authorize the use of the i-ballot throughout the country from 2019, in which case it would rapidly move up the *how* line.

So far we have focused on the *how* line. In the next chapter we'll look more closely at the *what*.

CHAPTER 3

THE EVOLUTION FROM WHO TO HOW AND WHAT

Just as the shift took place on *who* can vote, and is now moving to the question of *how* we vote, a shift is simultaneously under way with regard to *what* we vote on. In the digital era, technology will accelerate this shift.

To get a sense of where this is heading, it is worth recalling the changes that took place with regard to *who* can vote. At every opportunity, the tendency has been for rights to be enhanced. Men without property got to vote. Slaves were freed and could vote. Women got to vote. Literacy restrictions were lifted. The voting age was reduced from thirty to twenty-one to eighteen, and now to sixteen in some countries. In 2012, the White House introduced an electronic petition portal, "We the People", where citizens as young as thirteen years of age could submit petitions. The latest trend is to look into granting the franchise at birth, with the argument that it is undemocratic to exclude such a large share of the population on issues that will affect them in the future. The call is for a trustee arrangement, in the same way that parents look after their children's other interests.[38] In short, the system is never static. It is becoming more representative, more interactive and more democratic. On observing a similar tendency in ancient Greece, Plato had written that democracy was characterized by a "forgiving spirit" that hands out "a sort of equality to equals and unequals alike".[39]

Unsurprisingly, therefore, if there is anything that a modern democracy can do to make it easier for the people to have their say, it will be done.

Of all the measures taken by the modern representative system to become more democratic, the most surprising is that it has countenanced a very significant increase in the number of direct consultations of the people, i.e. on *what* people should vote. That is to say, rights have been extended to people to collect signatures to launch initiatives that the whole country can vote on. There have also been changes to constitutions making it compulsory in certain cases to get the people's consent. And there has also been a big increase in "optional" and "non-binding" referendums.

The reason why this is a surprise is that everywhere and always, such moves are evidence that something cannot be decided by the representatives alone – it is an admission of the imperfections and limitations of the representative system. Here we go back to an age-old problem: If the people are sovereign ("We the People"), then what is the function of the representatives in a legislature? What is their job? Given that the law merely represents the general will, Jean-Jacques Rousseau wrote in 1762 that no one can "represent" the people's law-making capacity. [40] Sure, the people can be represented in an administrative sense, the way a policeman enforces the law or a customs official levies a tax, but those officials are merely implementing what the people have decided. To hand over power to a parliament of representatives, Rousseau argued, is to place chains on the people for the duration of the life of that parliament. The chains are removed at the time of the general election, he claimed, only to be clamped on again the moment the newly elected representatives take their seats.

That a less than perfectly harmonious relationship can exist between a free, sovereign people, on the one hand, and a body of infrequently-elected representatives, on the other hand, is self-evident, therefore. The question is what should be done about that imperfection? The answer, it appears, has been to try and loosen the people's chains in the years *between* the general elections. The representative system is becoming "more democratic" in a new way – not by extending the franchise to more categories of citizens – that has already happened – but by permitting enfranchised citizens to decide on issues in the periods *between* the general elections.

Let's first take a look at the data underlying this trend. There has been a steady rise in national (i.e. country-wide) referendums and popular initiatives across the globe since records began in 1792 (thirty years after Rousseau made the argument), with a particularly marked increase since the 1970s and a further acceleration since the 1990s (Exhibit 2).

EXHIBIT 2: THE NUMBER OF COUNTRY-WIDE REFERENDUMS, FROM 1792 TO 2016[41]

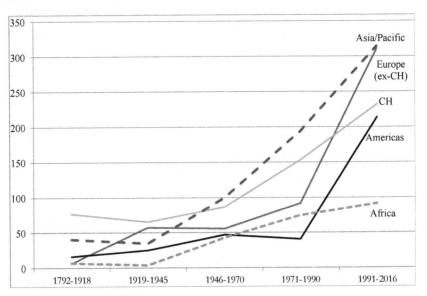

The difference between the term "referendum" and "initiative" is that the former tends to be used to describe the kind of plebiscite that comes to the people from the top, and the latter is where the people can trigger a vote on their own. Adding up all the data points that appear in Exhibit 2, we get the following breakdown:[42] 146 national referendums and popular initiatives in the period from 1792 to 1918, increasing to 186 from 1919-45, to 331 from 1946-70, a significant jump to 551 from 1971-90 and then a very substantial leap to more than 1,161 from 1991 to 2016. This means that the pace of referendums at the national level has picked up from an average of one per year from 1792 to 1918, to forty-six per year from 1991 to 2016. This latter period coincides with the fall of numerous authoritarian regimes and the spread of democracy in many places.

The biggest chunk of the 1,161 countrywide referendums since 1991 – almost sixty per cent – has taken place in Europe, more than a quarter in the Asia-Pacific region, one-fifth in the Americas, and around ten per cent in Africa. Compared to 1971-90, the biggest increase in the use of referendums has been in the Americas (an increase of 430 per cent), Europe (an increase of 240 per cent when *excluding* Switzerland because that country used to have the most referendums and would distort the number for Europe), Asia-Pacific (sixty per cent more) and Africa (an increase of twenty-five per cent).

Each region has had its own particular drivers for this increase. In Europe, we have to divide the referendum countries between "Europe (excluding CH)" and "CH", with CH being the official country abbreviation for *Confoederatio Helvetica*, or Switzerland in Latin. This territory in central Europe, which formed part of the northern border of the Roman Empire, beyond which lay the Germanic tribes, has held over six hundred nation-wide referendums since 1798. That equates to about one-quarter of all national referendums held worldwide. The big surprise is that, since 1991 Switzerland has been overtaken by the rest of Europe in terms of the number of referendums held: 311 in Europe excluding CH, compared to 232 in Switzerland. In the period 1971 to 1990, the numbers were 91 for Europe excluding CH and 153 for Switzerland. So, something is stirring in Europe outside of Switzerland – even before the switch to a digital voting system.

One key explanation for the increase in referendums in Europe is that the project to build the European Union has disturbed the centuries-old relationship between citizens and their local representatives. The EU caused sovereignty to be "pooled", requiring previously autonomous parliaments to download and rubber-stamp directives made in faraway EU "councils". Of course, a country was always represented in those EU councils, but some of the compromises reached there were not always popular when they had to be explained back home. Some of these changes started triggering referendums, resulting in a spillover to the neighbours. More significantly, the EU project has resulted in more countries formally incorporating legal provisions for referendums, including in Finland (1987), Portugal (1989) and even in two traditionally anti-referendum countries: the UK (2011) [43] and the Netherlands (2015). [44] The Netherlands, in particular, is an example of how the referendum genie has spread in Europe to encompass even non-EU topics. In the Netherlands, numerous state commissions in the twentieth century looked into the issue of whether the Dutch constitution should be amended to allow for referendums, but nothing much came of those efforts until the twenty-first century. [45] In 2004 and 2005 several European countries announced that they would hold a referendum on a new treaty for a constitution for the EU. Pressure grew for a referendum in the Netherlands, too, where such a type of consultation had last taken place 200 years earlier. The Dutch referendum contributed to torpedoing the new EU treaty for the whole of Europe – the deal required unanimity. Having tasted the power of the referendum, and with only one per cent of those surveyed having a "great deal" of confidence in the Dutch parliament in 2012, [46] further pressure to consult the people on more things subsequently led to the introduction of a new referendum law that allows citizens to *initiate* a referendum on certain acts and treaties signed off by the legislature, but before they come into effect. This is an example of how the representative system is trying to respond to the demand by the people for more say on more things in the years between elections.

In Italy, where the 1948 constitution gave the people the right to trigger referendums to abrogate certain types of laws, it was not until two decades later that the legal mechanism for this instrument was set up. Clearly, the Italian legislature was in no rush to allow the people to challenge it, even if the people had been given that right in the constitution. Once the people had the power to start challenging their legislature, they used it. There were three referendums in the 1970s, ten in the 1980s, thirty-four in the 1990s and twenty-three since 2000. Once Italy shifts to an internet-based system to collect signatures for initiatives and to vote over the internet, the number of initiatives will almost certainly rise at a faster pace.

Even in the UK, a country with a long tradition of representative democracy, the evidence is that the parliamentary system is being eroded by consulting the people directly on more issues more frequently than in the past. While that country had no nation-wide referendums before 1975, since then it has had three. And at the sub-national level, the UK has had nine since 1973. The people have turned out in droves for those consultations. Scotland's referendum in 2014 on whether or not to break away from the UK brought out eighty-five per cent of registered voters – the highest turnout in the country's history. In the 2016 UK referendum on whether to remain in the European Union, seventy-two per cent of registered voters participated, compared to sixty-six per cent in the 2015 and 2010 general elections. This increased participation rate of six percentage points means that three million people more felt the issue was important enough to get to the polls compared to the 2015 general election.

Stirrings at the sub-national level can spill over to the national level. In Europe's largest economy, Germany, opinion polls show that more than eighty per cent of Germans are in favour of the introduction of referendums at the national level.[47] This follows the introduction of initiatives and referendums at the local level throughout Germany since the 1990s. There have been around sixty referendums at the Länder-level since 1991, twice as many as during the period from 1950 to 1990.[48] The frequency of referendums is, therefore, also picking up in Germany. As of 2016, some eight thousand initiatives had taken place at the communal level and around three hundred at the level of the Länder. Germany has become a hotbed of people's power.[49]

In the Asia-Pacific region there have been over 300 referendums since 1991. Most of these have taken place in small island states.[50] In New Zealand citizens were given the right to initiate a referendum in a 1993 law if ten per cent of the electorate signs a petition. That will prove to be a low hurdle when the collection of signatures goes electronic. In theory, the referendum result is "non-binding" on parliament. But as we saw in the case of the "non-binding" Brexit vote in the UK and the "non-binding" 2016 referendum in the Netherlands on a treaty between the EU and Ukraine,[51] legislatures are facing an identity crisis. Are they in charge or the people? In both the UK and the Dutch case, the government decided that "non-binding" actually meant "binding".

As has happened elsewhere when new referendum tools have been introduced, there has subsequently been an increase in referendums also in New Zealand, from six before 1991 to ten since. Close by, Australia had been created via referendums in its constituent states. It was, therefore, thought wise that what had been created by the people via referendum should probably also best be amended by the people through that same instrument. Australia thus departed from the Westminster parliamentary tradition by adding this feature. Accordingly, forty-nine nationwide referendums were held between 1898 and 1991. But, whereas the number of referendums has exploded in the rest of the world, Australia has bucked the trend in that only two have been held at the federal level since 1991. The most obvious reason for this is that, until recently, there were no constitutional reasons to use this mechanism. The last referendum, in 1999, was on whether the country should become a republic. The people said "no". But in 2016, we saw what appeared to be Australia possibly starting to follow the global trend of asking the people to decide on more things. The Australian prime minister proposed holding a "non-binding" referendum on whether the country's marriage laws should be amended to permit same-sex marriage. The opposition voted to block the bill on the argument that a referendum was not the right tool via which this issue should be decided. This case also illustrates the dilemma of modern legislatures in democracies: On the one hand, they no longer feel competent to distil the view of the people they represent (the original reason why representative government was supposedly a superior form of democracy for our age); on the other hand, they are not prepared to trust the people to make the decision either, hence the "non-binding" disclaimer – just in case the people provide the "wrong" answer. Be that as it may, it seems unlikely that this is the last we'll be hearing about the radical idea that the Australian people should be consulted directly on new kinds of things.

Asia is a regional outlier in that no nation-wide referendums have occurred among some of the larger countries, such as China, India, Indonesia or Japan, but there is evidence of some stirring here too. In Japan, a law came into force in 2010 setting out the process by which mandatory referendums could be held so that the people could vote on any change to the constitution.[52] It took Japan over sixty years to reach that step. We should now expect to see the first nation-wide referendums in Japan. What has happened at the national level is, inevitably, also a reflection of an increase in consulting the Japanese people at the local level on more things. There was an increased demand for referendums in the 1980s and 1990s at the local level in Japan. The first local referendums there took place in 1996, resulting in a flurry of popular initiatives since then. Japan is a further example of the trend towards deferring to the people on more issues.

There is, however, no evidence of this contagion having reached China or India *at the national level*, but experiments in consulting the people directly are occurring in some regions. In Hong Kong, an unofficial referendum in 2014 drew nearly 800,000 voters – about a tenth of the population. An attempt was made to hold a referendum in Macau that would have included online voting, but that failed after the arrest of the organizers.[53] The reason given for the arrests was that in order to do the online vote, participants would have needed to supply their identification and mobile numbers. The authorities claimed it was a violation of data protection laws for a polling group to collect such data. These types of popular initiatives in which the people are not afraid to identify themselves using their IDs and mobile numbers are the most dangerous ones for an authoritarian regime because the state cannot arrest everyone.

The UK's Brexit referendum resulted in the spillover of some revolutionary thoughts in faraway places. In India, the Chief Minister for Delhi, Arvind Kejriwal, demanded a referendum on full statehood for Delhi. He was not put off by the fact that India's constitution currently makes no provision for a referendum.[54] Constitutions can be amended.

The UK Brexit referendum, therefore, represents a radical ripple that has spread out. Note has been taken that the British people were asked to decide something important, and that, despite the beseeching of their prime minister, the warning of the president of the United States that they would have to get to the back "of the queue" for a future trade deal with the US (implying that the script had been written in London because Americans would not use that term), and an official G20 statement warning that if the UK left the EU it would represent a global economic "shock" (again suggesting that the sentence was written in London because G20 members need to agree on the text), the majority of the British people ignored all that expert advice and voted to do the exact opposite.

Elsewhere in Asia, Taiwan suddenly had several referendums in 2004 and 2008 – on issues that its legislature evidently did not feel competent to decide on without guidance from the people. In Thailand the first nation-wide referendum took place in 2007, and then again in 2008 and 2016 – evidence of a political legitimacy problem. Other countries in the region that have had referendums since 1991 include the Maldives (five times) and Myanmar (on a new constitution in 2008). In South Korea, a referendum took place in Seoul on a proposal for free school meals (2011).

The trend to consult the people directly on more things has reached Asia, therefore. At the national level, it is still very much a top-down affair though. But the frequency of these types of consultations has increased.

In the Americas, as Latin America became more democratic in the 1980s and 1990s, there have been 209 referendums since 1991, compared to thirty-six in 1971-90 and just fifteen in the period 1792 to 1918. The most frequent users of this instrument in Latin America have been Bolivia, Chile, Colombia, Ecuador, Uruguay and Venezuela, but there have also been referendums since the 1980s in Argentina, Brazil, Costa Rica, Guatemala, Haiti, Panama, Paraguay, Peru and Suriname. Many referendums related to constitutional reforms, but also to a range of other topics, including trying to kick out a president in Venezuela and to prevent one from overstaying his welcome in Bolivia. A recall vote on President Chavez of Venezuela took place in 2004: on a turnout of seventy per cent, nearly sixty per cent reportedly voted against. In 2016 another attempt was launched to remove the president, Nicolás Maduro. So, once the people have a tool, they'll keep using it. And if they can collect signatures via their mobile phone, they'll use it even more. In 2016, the people of Bolivia turned down the request of their president, Evo Morales, to change the constitution to let him run for a third consecutive term. On a turnout of over eighty per cent, fifty-one per cent of the people voted "no".

The bigger countries of North America have been outliers when it comes to national referendums. Canada has held only three nation-wide referendums (on prohibition in 1898, on conscription in 1942 and on constitutional reforms in 1992). Canada nearly broke up in 1995. On a turnout of nearly ninety-four per cent, Quebec decided to remain by a vote of just over fifty per cent in favour.

The United States has never had a nation-wide referendum because that right does not exist in its constitution. There have been a few attempts to amend the constitution to add that right, but those attempts have failed. The story is very different one level down, at the level of the states. Currently, twenty-six US states offer such an instrument (Exhibit 3).

EXHIBIT 3: THE NUMBER OF US STATES ADOPTING SOME FORM OF STATE-WIDE REFERENDUM POSSIBILITY[55]

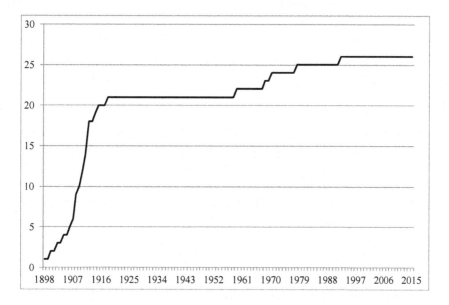

Between 1898 and 1918 several US states introduced referendum rights because advocates at the time saw the legislatures as beholden to powerful economic interests.[56] A reason why this instrument did not spill over to other US states in the south and the east in those early days might have been the fear that it would give too much influence to immigrants and African-Americans. [57]

The number of state-level ballot measures in the US (Exhibit 4) has increased from around six hundred in the period from 1902-18 to *over three thousand* from 1991 to 2016. This suggests a similar pattern of growth as in the case of countrywide referendums in the rest of the world, namely that the people are being consulted more often on more issues.[58]

EXHIBIT 4: COMPARING THE NUMBER OF STATE-WIDE
    BALLOTS IN THE US WITH COUNTRY-WIDE
    REFERENDUMS IN THE REST OF THE WORLD[59]

	1792-1918	1919-45	1946-70	1971-90	1991-2016
Rest of world	146	186	331	551	1161
% change		*27%*	*78%*	*66%*	*111%*
US states	613	1184	1163	1704	3233
% change		*93%*	*-2%*	*47%*	*90%*

Issues of popular interest at the state level have the possibility of making it to the national agenda and eventually influencing the policies of the entire United States.[60] That being the case, it is conceivable that as the collection of signatures for local initiatives switches to electronic platforms, it will become much easier and cheaper to launch initiatives in more states that offer such a right, on issues that also have national significance.

In Africa, a vast continent with big cultural differences between countries, there has been a sharp increase in the number of referendums. Eleven were recorded before 1945. Following a wave of democratization, the total number of referendums recorded stands at 219, with forty per cent of that number having happened since 1991.[61] In Africa it is now possible to find the full range of referendum options, including mandatory referendums, optional referendums, citizens' initiatives and the possibility to recall the president. These rights are not equally spread throughout the continent though. There are countries were none of these rights exist in the constitution and which have never had a referendum, and others that mention several of them.[62] The growing use of mobile phones in Africa (772 million mobile phones in 2016)[63] for payment services and as a source of information, suggests that we should not be too surprised if an African country turns out to be part of the first wave of countries to introduce binding votes via mobile phones.

In the Arabic countries of North Africa and the Middle East, a region not known for its democratic credentials, sixteen referendums have been held since 2000.[64] The significance of this trend is that it underlines the point that, increasingly in authoritarian regimes, rulers need to publicly uphold the principle that political power ultimately derives from the people. That was not the case across thousands of years of history, when rulers claimed authority by divine right or blatantly by the power of the sword. But, today, even in a theocracy like Iran, the constitution states that the country's form of government "has been endorsed by the people" *in a referendum*.[65] So, we have it in black and white that political power in Iran derives from the people. That constitution also states that what was created by the people by referendum also needs to be changed by the people via referendum.[66] In addition, the constitution permits the Iranian people to become *legislators*: for "extremely important economic, political, social, and cultural matters, the function of the legislature may be exercised through direct recourse to popular vote through a referendum". [67] Iran is constitutionally ready, therefore, for the people to start legislating from their mobile devices on "extremely important" matters, although no one could have imagined such a scenario when that text was drafted in the pre-digital world of 1979.

The danger of we-the-people constitutional texts in authoritarian settings is that, one day, the people may actually collectively assert that right. When, in 1989, the citizens of East Germany started marching down the street shouting "Wir sind das Volk" (We are the people), it was game over for a regime that did not have a reply to that one-liner.

Referendums are increasing in authoritarian regimes as well, therefore, because their constitutions claim that power derives from the people. It was easier to steer the outcomes of those votes in the era before mobile phones and the internet. Consider the case of the referendum in Iraq in 2002 in which the Iraqi people were asked whether they wanted Saddam Hussein to be their president for another seven years. According to the official election results, every single vote was "yes"— a turnout of 100 per cent in favour.[68] In the digital age, it would take just one person to post a selfie of themselves with their ballot to invalidate that result. In the digital age, it is a lot harder for a tyrant to control each and every citizen's access to a mobile phone. In the digital age, the we-the-people texts in constitutions can challenge what was thought to be settled law.

In many places, therefore, the people are being consulted on more things more often because old constitutional texts say they are actually in charge and more of them now have the audacity to start testing that assertion. Technology will facilitate and speed up what was already under way: Well before the introduction of the i-ballot, which will allow the people to vote in binding elections from anywhere, a clear trend was under way in dozens of countries across all continents to formally involve the people directly in making the law. The data shows a marked increase in the use of this direct involvement in recent decades, and on a wide variety of issues. The legislatures are deferring to the people on more issues more frequently, i.e. they are asking the people to decide policy directly. Consider the range of questions the people have had to decide on in recent years: on Brexit in the UK, on an international treaty between the EU and Ukraine in the Netherlands, on a new constitution in Thailand, on a peace deal in Colombia, on a new flag in New Zealand, on creating a senate in the Ivory Coast, on the opposite: taking away power from the senate in Italy, on immigration policy in Hungary, on holding the Olympic Games in Hamburg, Germany, on justice and the police in Denmark, on firearms in Brazil, on extending the president's term in Bolivia, on public funding for political parties in Bulgaria, on twenty-nine amendments to the constitution (twenty-nine separate votes!), in Azerbaijan, on ending conscription and introducing a professional army in Austria, on same-sex marriage in Ireland (yes), Bermuda (no), and in twenty-one US states, including in Maryland, Maine and Washington (yes) and in Minnesota and North Carolina (no). Across the globe, therefore, the people are now deciding on all kinds of issues directly. The evolution in terms of *what* we vote about is well under way. That momentum is about to be given a boost as the intervention of technology takes us further and further away from the representative model of the late 1700s.

CHAPTER 4

REAL-TIME KNOWLEDGE AND REAL-TIME POWER

The old version of representative democracy is eroding. An increasingly well-connected citizenry, that is testing the boundaries of the we-the-people slogans in constitutions, is less and less awed by its representatives. This is changing the power relationship between citizens and their representatives and underpins the shift with regard to *what* we are voting about. Technology is speeding up this transition.

On 4 April 2016, six per cent of a country's population suddenly and unexpectedly arrived in protest outside the legislature. This caused the prime minister to resign the next day, before the scheduled really big protest was to take place. The country was Iceland. The trigger? The prime minister's name had appeared in the so-called "Panama Papers", leaked documents about business entities registered via Panama. There's nothing illegal about an off-shore registration. However, following the global financial crisis, during which Iceland had suffered a collective trauma, this new information played into the narrative that those in power have additional ways to hide their wealth, tax obligations and conflicts of interest. It didn't feel right. The outcome was the de facto removal of a democratically-elected serving prime minister. This crowd had decided that his mandate was over.

In the digital age, things can go viral at the speed of light. This was not the first case in which information on the internet had brought out the crowds and caused a government to fall. The first case in which a government was toppled because of messages that appeared in the internet occurred in Tunisia in 2010. The trouble started after a foreign news portal reported on memos on Wikileaks by the US Ambassador to Tunisia. The specific details, including that the ruling family had their food delivered to them directly from France, added fuel to the fire. From there, the so-called Arab Spring protests spilled over to several countries in the region. Where they did not bring governments down, the protests resulted in governments suddenly handing out lots of cash and introducing reforms. Thus, it was no coincidence that shortly after the outbreak of the Arab Spring, Saudi Arabia's King Abdullah issued a decree that women would be able to vote for, and run in, municipal elections and that they would also be eligible to become members of an advisory council. There is nothing like an existential threat to focus minds on the elephant in the room.

People power was not invented in the internet age, of course. Almost two and a half thousand years ago, Plato had written that, "when assembled", the people are "the largest and most powerful class in a democracy."[69] The people, "when assembled" can also turn out to be very powerful in less democratic systems. History records that from the times of ancient China and the pharaohs, monarchs have been deposed on 1,114 occasions.[70] The mechanics of the loss of power include "murdered", "forced to flee", "overthrown", "forced to abdicate", "assassinated", "abandoned by his people", "captured in war and executed", "deposed and blinded", "deposed and strangled in prison", "head chopped off", "forced to cede", "died in exile", "partially deposed", "ceased to be king", "fled", "ceased to be queen", "removed" and "replaced". When the circumstances were right, whether by means peaceful or violent, the people have ended many a ruler's mandate. Clearly, that memo about the divine right of kings was ignored often.

While the internet was not required to trigger revolutions during the past five thousand years, today it would be hard to imagine an uprising that did not involve the internet in one way or another. Citizens now have it a lot easier than before to challenge their representatives via the internet, which is why authoritarian governments fear it.

Beyond their new-found technological capability to broadcast political messages far and wide, the internet has made the people more powerful because they now know so much more about everything in real time. This turns the representative model introduced in the late 1700s upside down. In the original version of that model, the representatives were supposedly the knowledgeable ones. They were the ones selected because they could be trusted to go to a far-away capital for several years at a time and deal wisely with the issues. But, since the people now collectively know much more in real time than any individual representative could ever know, the internet has shifted *de facto* power away from the representatives to the people. *De facto* is not yet *de jure:* legally the representatives are still the superior class. But where *de facto* leads, *de jure* is likely to follow. One bit of evidence for this comes from a precipitous decline in the people's confidence in the representative class (Exhibit 5), i.e. in that group that is still being elevated above the people via superior *de jure* powers.

EXHIBIT 5: A GLOBAL DECLINE IN CONFIDENCE IN THE
           LEGISLATURE
% of respondents saying they have a "great deal" of confidence in their national legislature[71]

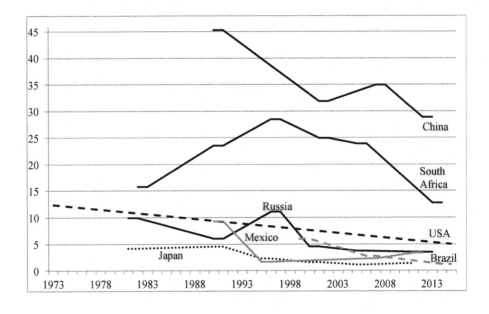

This decline in confidence is in stark contrast to the way things were supposed to be when the representative system was designed a few centuries ago. Gravitas and power – sovereign power, the power of the people – are what the chambers that house the legislature are meant to project. That was a long time ago. In 2015, in the year before the Brexit referendum, sixty per cent of the British people said that they "tend not to trust" what is decided in their own august legislature, housed in a *palace* called Westminster. [72] The Capitol, where the US legislative branch is housed, is awe-inspiring. Yet, the percentage of Americans who had a "great deal" of confidence in what goes on in that impressive building has declined from fifteen per cent in 1973 to just four per cent in 2015[73]. In Brazil and Japan the equivalent numbers have fallen to around one per cent.[74]

In countries that have moved from an authoritarian regime to more openness, the people appear hugely disappointed by their legislatures, no matter which party got in. In Hungary, which arguably has the grandest and most impressive parliament building in the world, confidence in what is decided in those chambers has collapsed from around fifty per cent in 1982 to less than two per cent by 2009. In Poland, it declined from twenty-four per cent in 1989 to a mere 0.2 per cent by 2013, in South Korea from twenty-four per cent in 1982 to three per cent by 2010, and in Egypt from close to thirty per cent in 2001 to around four per cent in 2012. A similar trend is under way in China: confidence in the decisions approved in the Great Hall of the People when the three thousand legislators meet there annually in the form of the National People's Congress, and in between as the smaller Standing Committee, has declined from forty-five per cent in 1990 to thirty-five per cent in 2007 and to just below twenty-nine per cent by 2012.

These trends tell us several things. The first conclusion from this data is that this is a global phenomenon. Almost everywhere, what their representatives are delivering for them impresses the people less and less. The second conclusion is that we are dealing with a trend that has continued over decades and across business cycles. This is not about the term of a single president or a single government – the representative system from the late 1700s is in trouble. The third conclusion is that it cannot be good news for the continuation of an arrangement whose *de jure* status ultimately rests on declining *de facto* legitimacy.

There is an analogy here with the disintermediation (cutting out the middle man) that has caused the grand, 200-year-old buildings that used to house stock exchanges, to go quiet. Today they contain no trading pits of significance – the job of the middle man is in decline. Buyers and sellers of securities connect via trading platforms. The analogy with grand parliament buildings is that technology can also eliminate the jobs of their middle men, the legislators. Political decisions can now be made directly by the people via an electronic platform. Technology, is not the hurdle.

The hurdle is a fear about what a society will look like when the people have a lot more power. What will a society look like when it starts implementing that "we the people" stuff that was written into the constitution three centuries ago?

We've been here before, and the lessons are not very encouraging. What we learn from the earliest democracies is that they did not survive: they had messy phases – they were suspended, amended, and ultimately scrapped. In Plato's *Republic* we read that it is almost inevitable that a democracy will morph into something less democratic because it contains the seeds of its own destruction. On the one hand, democracy was "noble" and "charming", but on other hand it was also characterised by "disorder". He wrote that democracies were places full of "freedom and frankness – a man may say and do what he likes,"[75] but that, ultimately, the "excess of liberty, whether in States or individuals, seems only to pass into excess of slavery…And so tyranny naturally arises out of democracy."[76]

Almost 2,400 years after Plato had written that, when democracies were imploding in Europe in the 1930s, Friedrich August von Hayek (1899-1992), who won the Nobel Prize for economics, tried to understand why the shift away from democracy was occurring. Hayek's conclusion was that "it is the ineffectiveness of parliamentary majorities with which the people are dissatisfied…the higher the education and intelligence of individuals becomes, the more their views and tastes are differentiated and the less likely they are to agree on a particular hierarchy of values."[77] That weakens the representative system.

By the end of the twentieth century and the beginning of the twenty-first, this apparent inability of parliamentary majorities to reflect what individuals want on a broad range of issues is a contributory factor to the falling membership of political parties, globally, and to declining levels of individual identification with a single party. [78] The representative system seems to be working well for fewer and fewer people. This erosion in its value means fewer people will be willing to defend it with their lives. Not surprisingly, therefore, surveys in the US in 1998 and 2016 showed that nearly a third of Americans would prefer government decisions to be taken by unelected officials.[79] In April 2016, a week after the Brazilian legislature launched impeachment proceedings against the president, only forty per cent of Brazilians thought that democracy was preferable to other forms of government.[80] When more than half the people think that a system other than democracy might be better, then it does seem as if Plato and Hayek may have been on to something.

But can it be true that we're becoming increasingly differentiated in our hierarchy of views and preferences? Certainly, the trend towards increasingly bespoke solutions with regard to almost everything appears unprecedented. Anecdotally, it has become almost impossible to be able to serve our guests around the table the same menu these days.

One objective indicator of the growing range of differentiation of views within society, and the impossibility for any single party to have the competence to deal with these, is the growth of issues covered by so-called non-governmental organizations (NGOs). In 1945, there were 41 NGOs granted "consultative status" with the United Nations. By 2016, that number had risen to 4,665 – still only a small share of the more than 24,000 NGOs in the UN's database.[81] Society is evidently coming up with more and more issues that are viewed as a priority.

Giving the vote to a single party to represent as many of these issues as possible does not appear to be consistent with the direction of increased differentiation into which we appear to be heading. Against this background, we can say that the representative system was in trouble long before the internet came along. The internet has just made things a lot worse for that model.

If today we had to explain to Plato why the internet is making things even worse for the representative system, we could use another one of Aesop's fables. Aesop is credited with the story about a lion and a fox. The fox had never seen a lion before, and so when she did for the first time, she was very afraid. The second time she saw him, she was still afraid, but not quite like the first time. And the third time she saw him, she had overcome her fear and went up to him to speak to him. The internet has reinforced the ordinariness of the representatives, and their lack of knowledge about our individual circumstances and our own hierarchy of preferences, which further undermines any claim they have to a special status to decide important matters on our behalf for years on end.

The internet has also undermined our representatives through overexposure. The Roman philosopher Apuleius wrote: "Familiarity breeds contempt, while rarity wins admiration." This principle is well understood in economics: if a central bank prints too much of its currency, money loses in value. In our modern world, the entire representative class has become like a devalued currency: they're in the media too often and they say things that are not relevant to our circumstances. Sometimes they even say things that are verifiably not true! Increased transparency – the internet – has undermined their status. It has led to a loss of awe for the representative class' knowledge and insight. Of course, it was never the case that the representative class in previous centuries was all-knowing and only made smart decisions. But in previous times the representative class was substantially shielded from the public. The people had only very limited insight into the day-to-day decision-making in the representative conclave. Only spectacular failings by the ruling elite, like the First World War, say, would give ordinary people the after-the-event evidence that their rulers did not always make wise decisions for the Motherland – and sometimes even made disastrous ones.

After the First World War, when the BBC first wanted to broadcast parliamentary debates, the British representatives refused.

Imagine that. The representatives of the people did not want the people to hear what they were saying in the debates in the house. They considered this to be too much of a risk. It took *another half a century* just to permit radio broadcasts, and a further two decades to allow the television cameras in.

From this we get a sense of the conclave-like protective cocoon that the representative system of leading democracies operated in until relatively recently. The people had their say at election time, after which the people went back to work, and the representative class conducted debates on the important matters of state, among themselves. The main points were summarized on the evening news.

We've come a long way since then. The people are now very, very close to what's happening in the legislature. What they see undermines the case for letting a group of representatives come up with superior solutions for the nation. The word parliament has its roots in the French word *parler*, to speak. Oratorical skills used to be important. That was then. But, these days, there is a website dedicated to violence in parliament, with categories including "Boxing and Punches", "Fireworks and Stuff", "Grabbing", "Guns", "Judo", "Kicks", "Slapping", "Strangling", "Throwing Water", "Using Chairs and Furniture", "Using Shields", "Men and Women", "Women" and "Uncategorized". [82] The site had clips from legislators from many countries. In April 2016, the violence in the Turkish parliament was so bad that the legislative process was stopped for two days to give the opposing sides time to cool off. In January 2017, it was the turn for violence exclusively between female members of the Turkish parliament. In Canada, the handsome prime minister, Justin Trudeau, was involved in a physical altercation on the floor of the Canadian House of Commons during which his elbow hit a female legislator in the breast, in what became known as "elbowgate". When even he is involved in violence in parliament, what is the world coming to?

In the US, the noble setting of the US House of Representatives was the scene of a twenty-five-hour sit-in by several members of the Democratic Party in June 2016. They violated various protocols, including that members should not sit on the floor, eat in the chamber or use mobile phones. A wonderful sight for visiting school kids. What would we think about a school that permitted the class to sit on the floor, eat in class and use mobile phones? When the official television feed was cut off, the members broadcast their own via social media. The spectacle reinforced the view of the helplessness of, at one point up to two hundred representatives. The unintended message was that these days, even if you get elected to the United States Congress, you don't have the power to change much – you have more power if you stage sit-ins and stream your protests via social media – like the people outside. Getting elected to the United States Congress is not where the power lies, is what they were showing us. It was not a strong endorsement of the representative system in modern America by the representatives themselves.

The "frankness" of democracy that Plato wrote about, which suggests it was always there, has been amplified in our digital age. In Greece, the economic crisis produced a surge of support for a "frank" political party, Golden Dawn. In 2012, twelve days before the general election, during a live television debate, the party's spokesman threw a glass of water in the face of a female politician opposite him (from the socialist party, so that's OK then) and slapped another female politician sitting next to him (from the communist party – even better). He subsequently received lots of Facebook "likes" from his supporters and got elected to parliament. Violence and abuse is prime time entertainment. The audience is drawn to it – and always was. The Coliseum used to be filled to capacity to watch the fights to the death between gladiators, slaves and animals. The whole purpose of public executions, from the days of crucifixions to other horrible ways to be put to death, was that the people could come to watch. People have been cruel and nasty to each other since the troubles started in the Garden of Eden. Later, even when the politicians had become gentlemen, they still fought duels for the purpose of killing their political opponent. By that benchmark, the violence and insults we see in parliament these days are toned-down versions of what our forefathers had seen or heard about. Things were far worse in the past – we are living in the gentlest of times.

Yet, unlike in the days of our forefathers, the internet has brought this behaviour into our homes, thanks to our mobile phones. George

Orwell had it wrong, therefore. The power to monitor has shifted from the government to the people. Greater transparency is not just undermining the credibility of the representative system in democracies. All representatives, whether they are elected by the people broadly or come to power by some other process, are exposed to its bite. In China, the representatives can no longer hide behind the walls of the Forbidden City. Chinese bloggers post photos of close-ups of the watches (and their prices) worn by officials.[83] That's a long way from the decorum and respectful distance shown to the emperors and statesmen in the paintings. When China's finance minister spoke in the Great Hall of the People in March 2016, some of the online commentary was very "frank".[84] The Finance Minister was subsequently replaced a few months later. Thus, when Article Two of China's constitution proclaims: "All power in the People's Republic of China belongs to the people", that increasingly means the people holding mobile phones. Now the lion has to be careful of the 1.4 billion internet-enabled foxes who might one day want to try the limits of Article Two.

We are heading into unstable times. The people won't behave.

Anecdotal evidence of the people's unhappiness with, and newfound lack of tolerance for, their representatives comes to us from many places. Brazil's president Dilma Rousseff was loudly booed when she appeared on the big screen at the opening ceremony of the 2014 FIFA World Cup. Using her wit, her explanation for the booing was that it came only from the rich people in the stadium who could afford the tickets. But that explanation appeared less convincing when she was impeached in early 2016. South Africa's President Zuma was booed in stadiums in 2013, at the memorial service for Nelson Mandela, in front of an audience that included world leaders, and again (in 2014) at an international football match. That booing was accompanied by the crowds making hand gestures indicating that it was time to change the player. A frank signal. Two years later, Zuma's party lost the biggest cities in local elections for the first time. President Barack Obama was booed in stadiums in the US in 2010, 2012 and 2014. The candidate that he was lobbying for lost the 2016 presidential election. France's President Francois Hollande was booed in 2013 at a ceremony commemorating the end of World War I, and in 2014 on Bastille Day. By late 2016, his approval rating had sunk to four per cent, and he subsequently decided not to run for the 2017 presidential election.[85] In Greece, the eighty-two-year-old ceremonial President of Greece, Karolos Papoulias, had to leave an event in 2011 commemorating the Second World War after the crowds started shouting "traitor" and the proceedings were cancelled. The foxes have lost their shyness. The volatile relationship between the *de jure* status of the representative class its *de facto* legitimacy, which used to be a private topic around the kitchen table, is now playing out in sports stadiums and live streams for everyone and anyone to see.

Is this loss of shyness a temporary blip? Should we expect the people to start becoming more respectful again of their representatives? Should we expect our representatives to start becoming more respectful to each other? Er, no. Things are not going to get any easier for the representatives in the decades ahead. There are a host of issues on the horizon that could give rise to a lot more frankness, and worse: be the trigger for a failing system to be replaced with something else.

In our digital age, there are three main economic sources of conflict that contain the seeds to substantially disrupt the status quo in western democracies. These are the conflicts between the winners and losers of *globalization, technological innovation* and huge *demographic shifts*. All three of these sources of conflict are going to have long-lasting effects, eroding a representative system as it struggles with issues that are unprecedented in scale and substantially beyond its ability to control.

The representative system is thus going to have to deal with issues for which there are no easy answers – and about which the experts disagree. A 2013 study found that forty-seven per cent of jobs in the United States could be replaced by computers,[86] whereas a 2016 report, using another interpretation, estimated only nine per cent.[87] The uncertainty about what the future economy will look like is huge. In a best case scenario, computers and machines will end up doing more work, whereas the people made redundant by those developments will find new and perhaps better things to do – which is kind of what has happened throughout history. A more challenging scenario for the representative system is when the jobs disappear before something new or better comes along – either because the applicants have the wrong skills and/or because the economy is simply not creating those new opportunities in sufficient numbers. If that were to happen, what kind of policies will the unhappy people vote for – especially if they can vote electronically about more things more often? Power is derived from the people, after all – that's what it says in those old constitutional texts.

To the extent that there has been downward pressure on manufacturing wages in developed countries and in certain categories of services jobs due to off-shoring and automation, this story, too, is far from over – and that will continue to pressure the representative system. Asia's population is projected to increase from 4.4 billion in 2015 to 5.2 billion by 2050, and Africa's population from 1.2 billion to 2.5 billion. That is the equivalent of another one-and-a-half-Chinas by 2050 in terms of the increase in population from Africa and Asia.[88] Such a huge increase in population will be the trigger for new wealth to be created by those who find the right products and services to supply these people, but it will also be the source of further pressure on those sectors that would suffer from this competition and for the new entrants into the global labour force. The globalization story is far from over therefore – it is just starting to enter the next demographic leg up.

What we don't know, though, is the extent to which technological innovation may end up replacing the new cheap workers from developing countries as well. If, in the future, there is less need for labour from these countries in manufacturing and in offshored services, then we may have many more regions with permanently higher levels of unemployment. That does not automatically result in chaos and revolution, but it can place an unreformed representative system in those countries under further stress.

Globalization, despite its current unpopularity in many places, is far from over, therefore, and has powerful forces driving it. In Africa, Asia and Latin America, efforts are under way to reduce barriers to the free flow of goods, services and capital among sub-sections of member states. In Europe, there are countries that have had years of discussions about getting improved access to the EU market (i.e. "more globalization"), including Albania, Bosnia and Herzegovina, Canada, China, Kosovo, Macedonia, Montenegro, Serbia, Switzerland, Turkey, Ukraine, and the United States. After Brexit, the UK says it wants to try that too. The discussions between the US and Europe to strengthen economic ties, despite the current opposition to those talks on both sides of the Atlantic, will reappear on the agenda again and again, because the demographic picture suggests that Europe will need to look for new market impulses in the decades ahead, and the US is not going to travel irreversibly along the road to autarky.

The future representatives will need to have the wisdom of Solomon to impress the foxes. That seems unlikely. In our digital age, lower hurdles to rebellion also have a physical dimension: things are getting more crowded. In 1950, the world's population was just 2.5 billion. By 2000, there were 6.1 billion people, and by 2050 the median forecast says there will be 9.7 billion, heading to 11.2 billion by the year 2100. We should expect more refugees and more displaced people and, therefore, more pressure on the representatives. And that is before we get to those other secular topics: water scarcity, energy and the environment.

Dealing with these known issues on the horizon using a representative model from the late 1700s does not seem to be a sustainable arrangement. Today we have the best-connected citizenry in five thousand years of recorded history. These citizens are becoming increasingly empowered through their access to real-time information. They will be less willing to defer to the lion – especially a lion whose policies are failing. The internet-connected foxes will be a lot less patient than the isolated and shy foxes in previous centuries.

CHAPTER 5

DEMOCRATIC DIGITS AND THE REDISTRIBUTION OF WEALTH

"the multitude is seldom willing to congregate unless they get a little honey"

Plato[89]

E verything that the people want from the state ultimately involves money. These demands can take on many different forms. Some people may want more of their own money as a result of lower taxes; others may want higher state spending on their preferred causes. In the digital age, people have more power than ever before to try to influence policy directly, including on the all-important questions of how the state taxes and spends. This is because it has become much easier for citizens to form digital alliances with like-minded communities, thereby boosting their lobbying power.

In the past, fiscal policy lay firmly in the gift of the representatives. The annual ritual of the British finance minister, the Chancellor of the Exchequer, walking out of his residence on budget day bearing a red briefcase containing information on the budget to be tabled in parliament, symbolizes the people's lack of power on fiscal matters in the old system. The people were merely spectators to an announcement about what the government had decided behind closed doors is best for them. In the US, the famous phrase "Read my lips: no new taxes" by George H. W. Bush in 1988, a promise that was broken two years later, illustrated that the people are not in charge of US federal tax policy, no matter who they vote for – the representatives are.

In the digital age, the additional leverage that the people are gaining will ultimately give them more say on more things, including on decisions related to taxing and spending. Consider, for example, the rise of the Tea Party movement in the US, with a focus on, inter alia, government debt, fiscal deficits and taxation.

At some point, a strong movement might arise that wants the opposite of what the Tea Party wanted. If people have more direct influence when it comes to fiscal policy, will this be a good thing or a bad thing? Will the people tend to be more fiscally profligate than the representatives or less so?

To try to answer this question, it is helpful, firstly, to know what happened when the representatives were in charge of fiscal policy. What do the historical taxing and spending trends show? On the expenditure side, they show a steadily increasing trend. Over time, the representatives have tended to spend more money on more things. Intuitively, that sounds right. It would have been surprising if the numbers had shown that the representatives had been spending less and less money on fewer and fewer things. The Nobel laureate Milton Friedman wrote eloquently about this.[90] He explained that this outcome was the inevitable result of a very normal behavioural trait: If we were given a pot of money to spend, wouldn't we also find good causes to allocate the money to?

Where does this pot of money come from? The long-term data shows an upward drift in the revenues that the state collects from taxes. This is not surprising because, over time, economies tend to grow. The US economy today is larger than it was a century ago. The same tax rate on a larger amount will produce higher tax income for the state. What is more surprising, though, is that there has also been a steadily rising income tax rate. In 1913, the lowest rate of federal income tax in the US was just one per cent and the highest rate was seven per cent. A century later, the lowest rate was ten per cent and the highest almost forty per cent. During emergencies, income taxes temporarily spiked much higher. In 1936, for example, the top income tax rate in America reached seventy-nine per cent. So, while the income tax rate can vary from time to time, the long-term drift has been up. When we multiply a rising tax rate with the growing amount of turnover in the economy, we get an even larger amount of revenue for the representatives to hand out.

Even more surprising than the rising tax rate is that the representatives looked for additional sources of income. When rising taxes were insufficient to cover expenditures, and the representatives did not want to risk becoming too unpopular by spending too little, they resorted to borrowing. Borrowing leads to debt. The long-term data shows an upward drift in government debt. In 1913 the level of US federal government debt stood at just eight per cent of the size of the US economy. Today it stands at 105 per cent of a much, much bigger economy. This means that the US system of representative democracy tolerated decades of federal spending that was higher than could be financed out of taxes, resulting in an upward drift in government debt. Wherever we look across the globe, a similar trend emerges: the representatives have allowed expenditure, taxes and debt to drift higher. Nowhere do we find a smaller, leaner state than a century ago. Moreover, based on what we currently know, there is going to be an on-going drift towards an even greater financial burden being placed on the state in the decades ahead. The single largest reason for this is the rising cost of the growing number of old people.

Throughout history, when money had to be found by the state to hand out, the money had to come from those who had some. In Plato's *Republic*, we read that "there is little to be squeezed out of people who have little...Do not their leaders deprive the rich of their estates and distribute them among the people...?"[91] As in ancient times, in our modern day and age, the representatives are not going to ignore the financial needs of a large and growing constituency of old people, out of whom "there is little to be squeezed". The number of people over the age of sixty-five in developed countries is projected to double between the years 2000 and 2050, to 340 million. In developing countries, a five-fold increase is projected, implying another one billion people in this age group.[92]

A close-up of this demographic shift in the US shows that the number of Americans over the age of sixty-five has increased from three million in 1900 (then just four per cent of the population), to thirty-five million in 2000 (twelve per cent of the population), and is heading to eighty-six million (twenty-two per cent of the population) by 2050 and 122 million (twenty-seven per cent of the population by 2100).[93]

Everywhere, older people – a powerful constituency of voters, supported by another powerful voting constituency, their ageing children – will probably vote for policies that provide more, not less, support to the aged. One can debate the extent to which younger workers will be willing to accept this transfer from themselves to the older generation, and the extent to which older workers will vote for this higher burden on their children and grandchildren. But these transfer debates rarely take place in a rational context free from financial pressure. We know from the recent debt crisis in Greece, where expenditure on state pensions had become unaffordable, that the outcome by 2016, compared to 2007, was a combination of cuts in pensions, higher taxes and a greater level of government expenditure as percentage of GDP than before the crisis. This means that, measured by its share of the economy, the Greek state actually became larger during the crisis! This also means that the financial burden on (younger) workers had increased. Greece has shown how difficult it is for a democracy to vote in a government that will dramatically slim down the size of the state.

For a broader category of countries, both rich and poor, the average additional expenditure on state pension schemes and state healthcare commitments represent perhaps an additional one hundred per cent of GDP by 2050.[94] For China the estimate is an additional $14 trillion for pensions and healthcare, for Germany $2.6 trillion and for Japan $2 trillion. In Brazil, additional government pension spending to 2050 is estimated at the equivalent of one hundred per cent of GDP and healthcare spending at sixty per cent of GDP when measured in today's money.[95] These are massive numbers. Unless a crisis breaks out first to make this a top priority, no-one is going to get elected on the basis of a promise to resolve that looming shortfall. No-one wants to talk about it. The story is very similar almost everywhere: the representatives have signed off on more social security than ever before to more people than ever before. That will be tomorrow's problem for someone else to sort out.

In the United States, federal liabilities and federal spending linked to these promises and the concomitant demographic changes have been projected to add another forty per cent of GDP in pension commitments and another 120 per cent on healthcare by 2050.[96] The US numbers mean that the US federal government needs to find funding for *an additional* $27 trillion on pensions and health care to 2050 ($6 trillion for pensions and $21 trillion for healthcare).[97] That is in addition to having to pay back (or refinance) the current $20 trillion owed by the federal government. Future representatives are going to have to find some really big pots of honey.

It does not, therefore, appear that over the coming decades we will be heading towards a smaller, leaner state, with lower government expenditure, lower taxes and lower debt. It appears, instead, as though we are continuing to drift towards future representatives having to find additional sources of wealth and income to tap. These trends become a lot clearer when viewed from a longer historical perspective. Writing in 1848, Marx could not have dreamt that the capitalist system he described would have evolved to provide the future proletariat with such a wide range of benefits, financed through a progressive tax and very large amounts of government debt. The revolution he predicted failed to materialize because the proletariat got the vote and used that power to opt for more redistribution.

The question now for us is where do these trends lead to in the digital age? The system cannot continue to allow government spending, taxes and debt to drift higher indefinitely. Or can it?

We have the answer from history. The answer is that the trends towards higher levels of government spending, taxes and debt will continue, until such time as they can no longer continue, and then they will be temporarily reversed, only to restart again at the earliest opportunity. This interpretation appears to be in line with what we know about the finances of ancient Greece and Rome, and also elsewhere since then.

The architecture, sculptures, art and literature of Ancient Greece attest to a very prosperous society. An epoch that produced Pythagoras, Socrates, Plato and Aristotle, contributed to mathematics, science and philosophy, and laid down principles of democracy and medical ethics, clearly had substantial income streams to support higher learning and the arts. Athens was, however, unable to sustain its income streams, and eventually went into decline. The growing welfare payments and subsidies in ancient Athens appear to have been "the real cause of the destruction of the noblest of all states known to history."[98]

Some five centuries after Plato had provided the view that "the multitude is seldom willing to congregate unless they get a little honey", the Roman writer Juvenal reported a similar problem in Rome: the only way to keep the people calm was for politicians to hand out "bread" and arrange "circuses".

Over five thousand years of recorded history, therefore, the financial story that keeps repeating itself across kingdoms and republics, large and small, is one of a build-up of sovereign largesse that eventually cannot be honoured.[99] The benefits are provided until, one day, they are abruptly stopped.

Will our digital age, in which the people have more say than ever before, be any different when it comes to fiscal spending? If the people are closer to the state's money levers, might we expect to see more fiscal prudence and a trend towards a smaller, leaner state, with a lower tax base, less expenditure and lower debt? Or might we see the opposite trend – towards the people pushing for an even greater redistribution of wealth?

History suggests it is more likely to be the latter.[100] Plato's pupil and colleague, Aristotle, described democracy as a form of government in which those who do not own much property, and are therefore in the majority, have the power. This is the key issue when it comes to the state's finances: Who has the power to decide on the redistribution of the honey? In the digital age, we will have an even more participatory form of democracy than in the days of Plato and Aristotle. In ancient Athens, typically more than half of the adult population did not qualify to vote. And those who did, had to appear in person to exercise that right. In the digital age, not only is the suffrage much broader (and getting even broader as the voting age falls further), but technology will allow the people to vote more easily on more things from anywhere.

There is a small possibility, however, that in our modern world we might be able to prove Plato and Aristotle wrong on democracies and fiscal excess; that, even in a democracy, the people will be gentle in squeezing for honey from those who yield the most, and reasonable in redistributing it. One potential way to try to do this is to grant the people, the shareholders who are funding the project, more power in determining how their money is being spent. At first this may sound counterintuitive – if the people have the voting apps on their phone, won't they authorize more government spending – even more than the representatives have been handing out? Not necessarily. The assumption is that we will be more careful in taxing and spending *our own money* than the representatives have been with other people's money. How can we have more say over what happens to our money? Several real-world options are available. One such option is something called "participatory budgeting" in which the people get to decide on the allocation of some expenditures. This idea has spread to many towns and cities across the world. The World Bank has studied the phenomenon[101] and there is even a global "participatory budgeting" map on the internet, which shows these towns and cities.[102] As one might imagine, there are advantages and disadvantages to opening up the budgeting process to the people, just as there are also advantages and disadvantages to allowing people to vote in a democracy. The key advantage to giving people more skin in the game through participatory budgeting, however, is that it introduces additional checks and balances on where the state's money is going. It is a lot harder for a politician to slip through an allocation to an expensive white elephant project when line-item approval is required by the entire electorate.

A different version of fiscal checks and balances by the people exists in Switzerland. This is a more extreme form of participatory budgeting, consisting of three key principles:

The first principle is that the people can control the representatives' ability to tax and spend because the people have the right to vote on any new taxes and expenditures at any level of government (federal, state, local). On the revenue side this includes the right to vote on the rates of income tax, value-added (sales) tax, corporate taxes, hypothecated taxes (i.e. taxes dedicated for a specific line item, such as roads) and inheritance taxes. The people can vote on who the taxes should apply to, and by definition, what exemptions there might be. The people's rights include the ability to propose new taxes, to veto the introduction of new taxes and to initiate votes on removing or reducing taxes. On the expenditure side, the people can veto line items, such as the purchase of new big-ticket items.

The reason why this freedom has not resulted in total fiscal chaos in Switzerland is because, even though the people have these powers, they seldom want to be bothered with this level of detail. But knowing that the people do have these powers, which they seldom use, makes the representatives think twice about what *might* trigger a popular vote that could sink the legislature's favourite expensive project. Knowing that the people might turn down a tax increase if it were ever put to them, helps to keep the tax increases moderate and infrequent.

The second principle the Swiss use is: stay close to the money. This means that the bulk of tax money is collected and spent close to where the people live: roughly one-third of the taxes go to the local municipality, one-third to the canton (state) and the rest gets sent up to the far-away federal government. In contrast, US government finances, as in many other countries, look like an inverted pyramid: most of the revenue and spending decisions happen at the top layer, far from the municipality. Returning the bulk of the revenue and spending authority closer to the people would shift the fiscal checks and balances closer to the people as well. This redesign might need to be introduced in other countries as a quid pro quo for handing more fiscal law-making power directly to the people.

The third principle is potentially the most controversial the world over. It should not be. A version was tried in the US at the federal level, but failed. A different version has been tried at the federal level in Germany and Switzerland, and (so far) it has worked. It is the principle that the state can spend as much money as it likes, but on one condition, namely, that it is able to pay for it without borrowing, unless there is an emergency. The Swiss have introduced a rule that requires the budget to be balanced "over the cycle". No-one quite knows what that means, but the legislators tend to defer to what the finance technocrats say the multiplication factor should be, and this approach has tended to produce conservative budgets (surpluses in the fat years). This rule can also be over-ridden in an emergency, of course. In fact, it is imperative that the rule can be over-ridden, because if it is too rigid, it will simply be amended away in the first emergency, never to return. By explicitly making an allowance to break the rule during an emergency, the law would force the representatives to get fiscal spending back on track when the emergency is over.

A meaningful fiscal rule would also make it less scary to let "the masses" start having more of a say on the budget. If new expenditures can only be implemented if they can be financed without resorting to new debt, then the people can help come up with proposals (and eventually decide) on where the money should come from. True, this contains a risk. But nothing is risk-free. The risk is that the people, who we learnt from Aristotle are not all wealthy, may vote for even higher taxes on the rich, as Plato explained. But as long as the system remains a democracy (both Plato and Aristotle questioned the survivability of a democracy), there will always be the possibility that the people could also vote to reduce both expenditures and taxes (i.e. reverse previous increases).

Giving citizens power to approve or veto government taxes and expenditures exists in a functioning state (Switzerland), and weaker versions of that exists in many towns and cities across the world. The outcomes so far have not been a disaster.

A close-up of the period from 1982 to 2015 shows that the US ran an average fiscal deficit of almost five per cent of GDP per year – a very, very large number over such a long period – while for Switzerland the outcome was around zero, i.e., a balanced budget over more than three decades.[103] The country with the large deficits had representatives, based in a far-away capital, in charge of expenditure; the country with the balanced budget had the people in charge, with spending decisions made close to where they live. In the US case, it is especially noteworthy that when the global economy was booming in the years before the 2008 financial crisis – the fat years – and money was flowing into the state's coffers, the US federal government was unable to set money aside for a rainy day. When the financial crisis hit, the US fiscal position subsequently deteriorated from an already bad place.

When people are asked to help decide how the government should live within its means, it gives them more skin in the game; it forces them to consider the alternatives, like getting back cash or spending it on a government project, and it brings home the reality that the state has limited resources. Giving the people more say over the budget is a risk worth taking when compared to the fiscal outturn delivered by the representative model between 1913 and 2017.

Needless to say, the Swiss balanced-over-the-cycle budget model is not perfect. The biggest problem with it is that it does not account for known expenditures way down the road, for example state promises linked to a rapidly ageing population. That problem is several cycles away, i.e. it will be someone else's problem to solve in another decade, and does not yet appear in this year's perfectly balanced cyclically-adjusted budget. Money is eventually going to have to be found for that – a lot of money. By 2050, the Swiss will have to find more than one hundred per cent of GDP for healthcare costs and perhaps another fifteen per cent of GDP on pensions.[104]

The way to address these faraway bills that will come due when today's politicians are safely retired, is to present the state's fiscal accounts in the same way that companies are required to do, so that we can see whether a company is solvent or not. Of course, governments are not companies, so a few tweaks might be necessary when drawing up the state's balance sheet. But not having any method in place to show the true fiscal picture will make matters a lot more volatile when the inevitable shock materializes.

Accordingly, as we move into the digital era, and citizens become empowered to vote on more things more often, we should have the courage to trust that the people will produce better outcomes with their own money than the representatives did spending other people's money. There is no evidence yet that the people will be consistently more profligate than the representatives have been. We should have the courage to let the people have a say on where the taxes should be levied, what the tax rates should be, and how the money should be spent. Technologically, this is now all very easy to do.

Let's take it a step further. If we can trust the people with greater decision-making power on how their own money should be spent, could we not also entrust them with having a say on protecting the value of that money? It keeps happening again and again that the value of ordinary people's hard-earned savings is wiped out by disastrous government policies.

When fiscal policy has been exhausted, i.e. the tax burden has become too great, the authorities turn to the same institution that has always faithfully come to the aid of its sovereign, the one that issues coin. Today, the biggest creditors of many governments are central banks. Historically, that kind of arrangement has not worked out well. Central banks are a branch of government. If the government refuses to pay them back, what are they going to do? Raise an army? That did not even work in the ancient world. In the period from 377-373 BC, eleven out of thirteen Greek states defaulted on loans from their lender of last resort, the Temple of Delos. When the auditors finally closed the books on the case, ninety per cent of the debt had to be written off. After that bad experience, it was thought safer to avoid lending to the sovereign and instead make loans to wealthy individuals, collateralized by land. That experience was so painful that, two centuries later this warning appeared in Ecclesiastes, Chapter 8, verse 12: "Lend not unto him that is mightier than thyself; for if thou lendest him, count it but lost."

For a long, long time after that, governments were not considered creditworthy. Hence they turned to other means to get money. The pressure on ancient Rome to spend was so great that the representatives resorted to the modern-day equivalent of creating fiat money, that is, money backed by nothing. The way fiat money was created in the ancient world was to issue coins with a higher nominal value than the value of the metal it was made out of. Thus, the Roman coin, the denarius, started out as a practically pure silver coin. It was so well known in the ancient world that it had its own currency symbol: X. Over time, the representatives reduced the silver content of the coin until, eventually, it was no longer made of silver. Its value subsequently declined from 1,050 to a pound of gold in 30 BC to 50,000 by 301 AD, and then rapidly to a hyperinflationary 2,120,000,000 by 350 AD.[105] The rich were initially able to protect themselves with a diversified portfolio of gold and land, but when Rome fell, and the new capital moved to Ravenna, they could not take their land with them. The poor then also lost their free bread and circuses.

And so it continued across the centuries: good times, followed by bad, and a lot of volatility. In the year 600 AD, interest rates in China, the inventor of paper money, were 72 per cent, with a low of 1.8 per cent in 1933, only to explode to 3,000 per cent by 1950.[106]

In the modern era, the United States pursued monetary policies that were often better than those in many other countries, but was itself not always a paragon of sound money. One indicator of the US's relative profligacy is that, between 1850 and 2017, the US dollar lost more than eighty per cent of its value against the Swiss franc. Another example is that on 5 April 1933 the president of the United States surprised the people by telling them to hand over their gold.[107] There were at least two well-documented cases when the president of the United States privately put the country's central bank under pressure to keep interest rates low, contributing to high inflation. The first episode resulted in inflation reaching an annualized 21 per cent in 1951.[108] The second episode, documented by tape recordings of private conversations,[109] contributed to a fifty per cent rise in consumer prices from 1970 to 1975.

A warning that the Fed's independence "is not set in stone" appears in Alan Greenspan's book *The Age of Turbulence* (2008). The general public is also not overly trusting of the monetary authorities. In a Gallup opinion poll in 2009, only thirty per cent of those surveyed thought the US Federal Reserve was doing an excellent or good job, the lowest level of support among nine federal agencies.[110] This anti-Fed undercurrent was highlighted during the 2016 US presidential election campaign when Donald Trump accused the US Federal Reserve of playing politics.[111]

Time and again, the representatives have struggled to restrain themselves from tapping into the central bank's honey pot. Here, then, is a reason why it might be safer to take responsibility for monetary policy away from the representatives and hand it directly to the people.

Central banks are seen as part and parcel of the government and they get to feel the pressure directly from the streets during crises. In Europe, the global financial crisis caused the people's trust in the European Central Bank to decline dramatically. In May 2015, only thirty-two per cent of Germans said that they tend to trust the ECB – way below levels in 1999.[112] In 2015, ten thousand protestors demonstrated against the European Central Bank in Frankfurt. The President of the European Central Bank, Mario Draghi, said that "the ECB has become a focal point for those frustrated with this situation."[113] The ECB got off lightly. The Greek central bank was bombed in 2010, 2014 and 2015.

But how realistic is it that the people could have a direct say on monetary policy? That depends on how the mechanisms are set up. It has already happened that the people have voted on narrow monetary policy issues. In a referendum, Australians rejected the proposal that their parliament should have the power to control prices. Several European countries – including Denmark (no), France (yes), Italy (yes), Ireland (yes), Sweden (no) voted by referendum on whether or not to change their monetary policy set up. In Switzerland, the people have voted on the question of whether their central bank should sever its link to gold (yes), sell its surplus gold (1,170 tonnes: yes) and hand over the cash (yes). A counter-proposal to try and stop a future raid on the central bank's gold was rejected by nearly eighty per cent of voters in a referendum in 2014. So, if the people are asked to decide on technical topics related to pricing mechanisms, monetary policy, gold reserves and their currency, they seem perfectly capable of delivering an answer. Of course, the answer might not always be the one that the experts might want to hear. But we also know that the experts are not infallible.

The possibility therefore, that in the digital era, the people might want to have an even bigger say on monetary policy is almost certainly going to be tried out somewhere. In all probability, such demands will arise following perceived big policy mistakes or some significant economic shock, from which "lessons" will be learnt about how the people should not have entrusted their representatives with so much power.

Since the global financial crisis, fiscal policy and monetary policy have become increasingly intertwined as a result of central banks buying large quantities of all kinds of things. The professionals have opened that door and created a precedent. In the digital age, the people will have the technological means to decide on more things more often. When they figure out that they actually own the central bank, they might just want to try their hand at monetary policy too – especially if they disagree with what is being done in their name. In 2009, demonstrators broke through a barricade at the South African Reserve Bank demanding an interest rate cut. They were modest. Imagine if they had known that they could actually have demanded something more powerful: helicopter money.

Central banks have shown that they are large pots of honey in difficult times, and have blurred the line between fiscal and monetary policy in our modern age. An additional loophole for the redistribution of wealth has been opened. That genie is now out of the bottle. In a future crisis, it will be hard to argue that the central bank cannot "help out" with a bit of honey. The question is who will be directing monetary policy then – the representatives or the people? We do know that when the representatives are in charge of monetary policy, especially in difficult times, we tend to get debased coins and higher inflation (sometimes even hyperinflation). The risk, therefore, that things could turn out a lot worse if the people were to have more direct say over monetary policy must be lower. The reason is that, in the same way that "participatory budgeting" increases transparency into the fiscal process and gives taxpayers more buy-in, "participatory monetary policy" would also substantially increase transparency about how decisions are made about the value of the people's money and, given the technical nature of monetary policy, would probably lead to prudent monetary rules and to more public checks and balances. Should the president, alone, be responsible for appointing his partisan buddies to the board of the central bank? Should a prime minister, alone, be able to order a country to hand in banknotes representing over eighty per cent of the money in circulation – as the prime minister of India did in 2016?

No doubt, outlawing the ownership of gold and other monetary assets will happen again and again – and always without the people's consent. "Participatory monetary policy" might protect us from such surprises. If the idea to confiscate the people's gold and money is so smart, then the representatives we elected to represent us on a broad range of issues should make the case to us on this narrow issue and let us decide if we agree. If not, history is full of examples of far worse confiscations that keep reappearing in the representatives' toolkit.

"Participatory monetary policy" might also help to prevent the loss of our assets through risky monetary policy experiments. The challenge that the central banks face in the aftermath of the crisis is huge. These are unelected officials whose policy mistakes can change the course of history. The Fed presided over a contraction in the quantity of money of about one-third from late 1930 to early 1933, and the collapse of forty per cent of the country's banks. The unemployment rate rose from three per cent in 1929 to twenty-five per cent by 1933. In 2008, the then Chairman of the US Federal Reserve, Ben Bernanke, admitted: "Regarding the Great Depression. You're right, we did it. We're very sorry."[114] Sorry? For causing the Great Depression? The monetary policy experts caused all those suicides?

Almost eighty years elapsed between that disastrous Fed policy and the apology. These days, social media would pinpoint the culprits a lot faster. The foxes are lying in wait.

We know, therefore, that central bank independence will not protect us from poor monetary policy decisions, and we also know that central bank independence is something that only exists on paper during the good times. It collapses in a really serious crisis – and some of those crises are inadvertently caused by central banks themselves.

As we move into a digital age in which the people get to decide on more things more often, sooner or later one of those things could well be about protecting the value of money. Some day somewhere, enough people will figure out that they own both the treasury and the central bank. When that discovery is made, it will come as no surprise to Plato.

CHAPTER 6

SHINING LIGHTS ON OTHER HILLS

Where do these trends leave the leader of the free world, the country that introduced the system of representative democracy in a republic in the modern era? Is the United States the country we should be looking to for inspiration for the next iteration of democracy – for (Representative) Democracy 2.0?

Surprisingly, this does not appear very likely for several reasons: The first is that the current US system has produced stable government *over several centuries*. We have seen a gradual approach to constitutional change in the US. If George Washington were to look down on the country today, he might be surprised to discover that the slaves have been set free and that blacks and women can vote, but he would also recognize that there had been no revolutionary change to the US system of representative democracy. That makes the United States the oldest, continuously-functioning democratic republic in the world. Against that impressive track record, there would obviously be a lot of reticence in the US to try out big new constitutional experiments, unless forced to.

The second reason why the US is unlikely to be an innovator in shifting power from the representatives back to the people is a fear of – or shall one perhaps say, a respect for – what might happen if a new arrangement were to draw in too many of the other half who typically don't vote. In most countries, citizens do not need to register to vote – their names automatically appear on the voter's role when they come of age. But, not in the US. Without further reform, the US has, therefore, effectively reached its own limits of representative democracy – its system is now "as good as it gets".

The lack of further political reform in the US will also have implications for America's leadership role in terms of extending political freedom to the rest of the world. One cannot be a leader if others are testing the frontiers of new ways to vote and new things to vote about.

Not being a leader for freedom is a change from America's traditional role. A little bit of context might be useful here – it will also help explain the title of this chapter. In 1630, a 42-year-old Cambridge-educated lawyer, John Winthrop, left England for the New World. Winthrop had invested a sizeable sum into a commercial venture in the vicinity of present-day Boston. Winthrop, who subsequently became the governor of his colony, is today best remembered for a much-quoted phrase that found its way into prominent speeches by John F. Kennedy and Ronald Reagan. He had inspired his fellow settlers with the vision that their new country would be "a city upon a hill" – a beacon for all the world to see. Long-term economic data shows that his forecast was spot on – up until 1999.

EXHIBIT 6: US GDP PER CAPITA AS A MULTIPLE OF GLOBAL GDP PER CAPITA, 1700-2015[105]

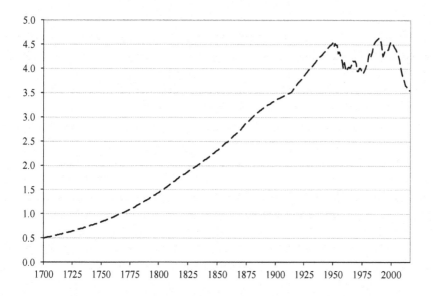

When looking at the US GDP per capita performance from 1700 to 2015 (Exhibit 6), relative to GDP per capita in the rest of the world, we see a pretty impressive story up until 1999, when things start to deteriorate for the US. To know why this is the case, we need to start before 1700.

A culture that emphasized the rule of law and individual liberty, combined with the availability of large expanses of inexpensive, open land, attracted millions of immigrants – and not only the poor. From the earliest days, the sophistication of the legal system in the American colonies attested to the hand of a learned and wealthy elite. We see this influence in many tiny details. A law that explicitly prohibited the taxation of income held offshore is probably not something that the average citizen would have come up with. Yet, a 1641 law in Winthrop's new home, the Commonwealth of Massachusetts Bay, permitted residents to keep their money offshore, tax-free. The relevant law stated: "No man shall be rated here for any estate or revenue he hath in England, or foreign parts, till it be transported hither."[116]

Relative to what was happening elsewhere in the world, the recipe that made America a rich country continued to work its magic over many centuries. The GDP per capita of the American colonies was around half of global GDP per capita in the early 1700s, reaching parity around the 1760s. By the late 1700s, a century-and-a-half after Winthrop had arrived in Boston, America had overtaken the world in terms of per capita income at a rapid pace.

By the early 1800s, US per capita income was *twice* the global level, and *three times* as much by the late 1800s. American wealth was being generated at an enormous pace, relative to the rest of the world. When American soldiers arrived in Europe for World War I, they were bigger than their European cousins, reflecting the greater abundance of food back home. American men who reached their eighteenth birthday in 1914 were taller than the median height for comparable groups of Dutch, German, French and British men. A century later, by 2014, the median height of eighteen-year-old American men was *below* that of the comparable European groups for the same countries. Now the Europeans seemed to have been better fed![117]

In January 1989 President Ronald Reagan delivered his farewell address to the nation. Drawing on Winthrop's analogy of the city upon a hill, Reagan asked: "And how stands the city on this winter night? ...after 200 years, two centuries, she still stands strong and true on the granite ridge, and her glow has held steady no matter what storm. And she's still a beacon, still a magnet for all who must have freedom, for all the pilgrims from all the lost places who are hurtling through the darkness, toward home."

Unbeknown to Reagan, the tectonic plates of history were about to shift. They would first propel America to the only super-power. But, within the seeds of the collapse of the Soviet Union and China's entrance into the global economy lay a new economic order which, combined with new technology, would free others in faraway places to start making money too.

With less darkness in the world, the lights of the original city on the hill became a little less exclusive among the many new bright lights popping up on different hills.

What Winthrop was looking for in 1630 – a place to practice his religion, freedom of speech, with strong property rights and reasonable taxes; a place to make money and accumulate wealth – all that, and much more, became available outside of America in more and more places.

The last two decades of the twentieth century coincided with the unleashing of market forces globally as large swathes of the planet opened up to the freer flow of goods, services and capital. Initially, this benefited America as its entrepreneurs had a first-mover advantage in selling their sought-after goods and services in newly-opened markets. This brought profits back to America, boosting US per capita income. At its multi-century peak, in 1999, America's GDP per capita stood at slightly above four-and-a-half times the global average. At no time since the discovery of America by the first Europeans in the 1500s had its residents been more prosperous, relative to the rest of the world.

Soon after 1999, though, things started to change, as the income gap between America and the rest of the world began to narrow. By 2015 it had slipped to three-and-a-half times. That's still impressive, but it returns the US to a relative position it last had in the 1920s.

The main trigger for this slide was initially external: increasing numbers of people in the rest of the world were finally permitted by their governments to play America's game, that is, to make money. Up until that time, the residents of the communist countries and much of the "third world" were essentially onlookers as the US and a few Western players delivered the goods, making themselves rich in the process. By 1996, sixty-eight per cent of the world's 192 billionaires were not US citizens. By 2014, that share had increased to seventy-two per cent of 773 billionaires. Or put another way, America had thirty-one fewer billionaires in 2014 than it would have had if the ratio had remained the same as in 1996. In 2014, some sixty-nine per cent of US billionaires had made their wealth themselves, as opposed to inheriting it, compared to seventy-two per cent in the rest of the world.[118] The rest of the world had become a hotbed of entrepreneurship and capitalism.

Given that there is a close link between economic freedom and the ability to find new ways to make money, the narrowing income gap between America and the rest of the world therefore also implied that there was an increasing level of economic freedom in more places. As individuals in the rest of the world gained more freedom, the gap between the freedoms which American society enjoyed relative to others had become smaller.

Whereas the US used to be the undisputed leader in people's rights and in being a stronghold of capitalism, gradually the US began to lose this leadership role. The newcomers had the advantage of being able to start with a clean slate. They had torn up their authoritarian constitutions, designed new ones and added additional democratic bells and whistles.

There is a range of ways we can track this narrowing "freedom differential" between America and the rest of the world. Initially, the US was almost always ahead of the others in extending rights to the people. One example of this trend would be extending the right to vote to women. Whereas the US was in a relatively exclusive club on this measure in 1920 – three to four decades ahead of most of the rest – this exclusivity continued to be eroded throughout the twentieth century. By the beginning of the twenty-first century, the overwhelming majority of the world's women over the age of eighteen had always been able to vote.

A feature of the "catch-up" process is that several of the latecomers ended up surpassing the original US achievement. Thus, once having enfranchised women, countries other than the US got the first female head of government. By 2015, fifty-two countries had had a female head of state.[119] Once they had female legislators, other countries exceeded the US share of female lawmakers. By 2016, the US House of Representatives ranked only ninety-fifth in the world out of 185 legislatures in terms of the percentage of lawmakers who were women.[120] The percentage of women in the US House of Representatives was nineteen per cent, more or less in line with the global average. The parliament with the highest share of female legislatures, sixty-four per cent, is to be found in Africa (Rwanda).

We see this "catching-up" with the US and "surpassing" the US in a broad range of areas. It was the awful state of human rights in England that the settlers in the American colonies left behind that inspired the 8th Amendment to the American constitution, forbidding "cruel and unusual punishments". At its apex, at the end of the 1700s, there were more than two hundred offences for which the death penalty was prescribed in England.

Over the years, England reduced the number of crimes for which the death penalty was reserved so that there is now no crime for which a person can be executed in England. This was the same story for over one hundred countries by 2015.[121] The United States is not one of them. Whereas the US led the world in terms of freedoms at the beginning of the 1900s, by the late twentieth century, one often had to look elsewhere for intellectual insights and practical case studies when it came to the extension of new rights to the people.

In argument before the US Supreme Court to legalize same-sex marriage in the US, evidence was presented of how this issue had been handled in South Africa, where the basis for these rights had been incorporated in that country's new constitution two decades earlier under the following sweeping article: "The state may not unfairly discriminate directly or indirectly against anyone on one or more grounds, including race, gender, sex, pregnancy, marital status, ethnic or social origin, colour, sexual orientation, age, disability, religion, conscience, belief, culture, language and birth." That's not the kind of clause that the US founding fathers would have come up with in the 1780s, but Nelson Mandela agreed to it in 1994.

And so it came to pass that same-sex marriages became the law of the land in parts of Africa, but remained illegal in cosmopolitan New York City until 2015. The US system, which used to be far ahead of anyone else in terms of the extension of civil liberties, had been overtaken by the tortoises. Now the US was playing catch-up.

The biggest surprise of all, though, is that the US would allow itself to be beaten at its own game on some of the fundamental rights it essentially patented in a modern society. Hayek described private property and the protection of property rights as "the most fundamental guarantee of freedom". According to the International Property Rights Index, which looks at the legal and political environment for the protection of physical and intellectual property rights, the United States ranked only fifteenth overall in 2015. According to that index, property rights were better protected in parts of Western Europe and the Asia-Pacific than in the United States.[122]

The Heritage Foundation's 2016 Index of Economic Freedom did not rank the United States among the top ten economies in terms of economic freedom.[123]

Freedom House's Annual Index of Media Freedom in 2015 ranked the United States in thirty-first place in terms of press freedom. The US Constitution's First Amendment (1787), which was revolutionary at the time, declares that "Congress shall make no law ... abridging the freedom of speech, or of the press". These days, however, many countries have similar laws, but apparently provide journalists with greater protection in not having to reveal their sources. According to this survey, freedom of the press is today ranked more highly in Europe than in the US.

Collectively, these differences begin to add up in relative terms: new cities on other hills that are better ranked in terms of economic freedom, property rights, and freedom of the press, are now also rolling out new technology by which citizens can choose and instruct their legislature. In contrast, the US is sticking to the model of the 1780s that has worked well for it.

This *relative* deterioration in the US position has been obscured by the blessing – some might call it a curse – that comes with being a big country. A big country is not typically concerned about "competitiveness" because it has such a large domestic market that can compensate for a loss of exports. A big country does not fear little states. One area where this is particularly noticeable is in the area of corporate taxes. Whereas the rest of the world had dramatically cut corporate tax rates to well below the US rate, the US corporate tax rate was unchanged from last century at an average of forty per cent when including local taxes – the world's highest in 2015. The average for Europe in 2015 was half the US rate. Clearly, the world had changed when the US had become the high income tax country. The high US corporate tax rate suggested a lack of focus on something absolutely fundamental to investors. It was the reason why so many US companies and investors retained money outside America. US companies held around $2 trillion in undistributed earnings abroad in 2013, money that was not taxed in the US.[124] It would have been very easy to bring that money back to America – just reduce America's corporate tax rate from the highest in the world. But the "big-country syndrome" meant that it was very hard for those in charge to recognize that the laws of competition apply to the US as well. Instead, the system misdiagnosis the problem as a lack of "loyalty", and tries to address the problem by punishing the "disloyal" and blocking the exit doors.[125]

The US, which had been the beneficiary of the largest and longest inflow of capital to any country on the planet, was traditionally welcoming of that capital. But whenever capital threatened to leave, or when it was discovered that the money was already out of the country in large amounts, then the system struggles with the notion that there can be brighter lights in cities on other hills. Ironically, this has resulted in the unintended consequence that people with money have been discouraged from moving to the United States by a series of laws that would severely punish them if they ever wanted to leave again. *The Economist* magazine referred to the new laws introduced in 2008 as "America's Berlin Wall".[126] Another US law creates a legal mechanism to ban former US citizens from America if the reason for giving up their citizenship was to avoid US taxes.[127] This means that you can give up your US citizenship, a costly and time-consuming process, but you should never officially let it be known that you are doing so because the city on the other hill gave you a better tax deal. Just to make it even less comfortable, US law requires that the names of all persons who had the temerity to give up their US citizenship should be exposed. Since 1996, when the law came into force, the names of 23,000 men, women and children have been published in the *Federal Register*, with almost one-fifth of that number recorded for 2015 alone.[128] Looking through the list, one wonders whether anyone voluntarily would have wanted to go through the emotional process of renunciation. But clearly, the costs of holding US citizenship had been rising for the wealthier, as had the attractions of the lights in the cities on the other hills. Few in Washington had noticed or appeared to think this was relevant. America is a big country after all.

While the US is known as a nation of immigrants, it is less well known that around 12 million people *emigrated out of* the United States in the twentieth century. In the first decade of the twenty-first century, emigration out of the United States was estimated at between 180,000 to 230,000 per year.[129] These may be negligible numbers for a big country, of course. But the point is that people are mobile and there are alternatives today.

The disadvantage of a big country, as prosperous and populous as the US, is that these trends appear minor or irrelevant – until, one day, suddenly they're not. A small country would nervously have picked up on them sooner. A good example of this big-country mind-set was the announcement by the Obama Administration in April 2016 to block the pharmaceutical company Pfizer, which was headquartered in the US, from buying a smaller competitor whose tax domicile was in Ireland. That so-called "tax inversion" deal would have lowered Pfizer's taxes. President Obama justified the new measures to prevent an outflow of capital by saying that: "They effectively renounce their citizenship. They declare that they're based somewhere else".[130] America in the second decade of the twenty-first century was not going to let the "disloyal" take their money out without a severe penalty. President Trump's pressure on companies to help "make America great again" by producing and investing in the country is consistent with the evidence in Exhibit 6 that it had become tougher for that relative wealth line to keep rising. The thought that money would flow back into America in huge amounts (without threats) if the representatives made the country competitive, did not make it through the "big country" filter. Competitiveness is for the midgets of Lilliput, not for Gulliver.

Little wonder, then, that the income gap between the US and the rest of the world had narrowed. With America no longer the only shopping mall in town, and with lower taxes elsewhere, there were now some pretty good competitors in the field who had discovered how to make money.

As the disruption by the forces of globalization, technology and demographic shifts make their presence felt in more places, America will probably lag behind when it comes to implementing ideas on how power should best be redistributed between citizens and their representatives. A system that has worked for two-and-a-half centuries, and that is still much richer than many other places, is not going to see any urgent need for constitutional reforms. Yet, given that the US is a federal republic with a lot of inter-state competition, including some states with direct democracy, one cannot rule out that no shift will eventually take place. Technology could also make it a lot easier to unlock Article 5 of the US constitution (1789). This article provides a way, never-before used, to change the constitution. The procedure is that two-thirds of the states ask Congress to call a convention to propose amendments, which become law when ratified by the legislatures or conventions of three-fourths of the states.

In 1789 the communication between state legislatures was slow. Today it is technologically possible to set up a live electronic voting platform between the state legislatures. Since America believes in "build it and they will come" – perhaps someone might come up with the idea to build that electronic platform and, once it is set up, test it with a few popular proposals for amendments.

In the meantime, for radical political reforms, we will need to look elsewhere, to the little ones, today's innovators.

CHAPTER 7

THE NEW HYBRID MODEL

Democracy has always been a dynamic arrangement. Plato wrote that in those parts of the ancient world where liberty reigned, there was "a complete assortment of constitutions" and that one "must go to a democracy as he would to a bazaar at which they sell them, and pick one out that suits him."[131] The question of who can vote, how they vote, when they vote and what they vote about, has differed from one democracy to another, and from one era to another. That differentiation continues to this very day. We do not live in the same democracy that our forefathers knew, and future generations are not going to stop coming up with new tweaks that will differentiate their rules from what we know today. Given this evolutionary feature of democracy, what are the clues about where this process might take us next?

We already see evidence that a shift is taking place in terms of *how* people vote (the people's instructions are going electronic, i.e. computers are playing a much bigger role in the transmission of ballots) and *what* they are voting about (a massive increase in the use of petitions, initiatives and referendums globally on all kinds of topics). The *frequency* of the interaction between the people and their representatives is picking up. The people are now online 24/7, and elected officials are tweeting to their constituents day and night – even on weekends. We arguably even had the first cases of *de facto* executive orders by tweet when Donald Trump, soon after his election as president, sent out messages about car factories, import levies and the prices of aircraft and pharmaceuticals, that moved the share prices of the affected firms. Democracy in the digital age looks like it is going to be materially different from democracy in the bronze age.

This *de facto* shift in power to the people in the digital age is slowly being reflected in *de jure* changes. Constitutions are being amended and laws rewritten to give the people more direct say on more things and to permit binding electronic forms of interaction.

Against this background, new ideas are being launched to propose tweaks to the old representative model. Some of these ideas have attention-grabbing names, such as "liquid democracy", "delegated democracy", "smartocracy", "viscous democracy", "structural deep democracy" and "emergent democracy", among others.[132] What these ideas all have in common is that they represent a form of power-sharing somewhere between the old representative model and direct democracy. In other words, we can classify them as a "hybrid" model that combines greater decision-making power for the people with some form of professional representation.

There are similarities in some of these proposals to what we know from a shareholder's meeting in which a shareholder can choose between being present at the annual general meeting or vote by post, or delegate the vote to a proxy. The difference to a shareholder's meeting, though, is that a shareholder would normally provide that proxy right to someone to vote on the entire agenda for the meeting as part of a pre-agreed package. In contrast, the new idea is to let the voter sign over proxy rights on many different topics as often as they occur, and to have the right to pick and choose on which of these issues the voter would prefer to decide directly.

Some of these ideas have also been inspired by the possibilities of the digital age, i.e. that it has become technologically easier for the people to transmit their decisions on more things more often. These proposals, therefore, go significantly beyond the powers and rights that shareholders typically have in most jurisdictions today.

These ideas also represent a decisive move away from the current representative model under which a voter hands over a blank authorization mandate to a single party for several years at a time and leaves it all to that particular party to sort out. Intellectually, that model looks to be pretty much over already.[133]

While there is a growing recognition that the representative model from the late 1700s is not going to survive the digital age unscathed, there is also an unease about making changes that are too radical and too fast at this stage. This reticence would explain some of the proposals that aim to give the people just a little more direct say by, for example, carefully grafting on an extra chamber to the current representative system. One such proposal is to establish a third digital chamber where draft legislation and budgets can be discussed online directly by the people.[134] Another proposal is to add a chamber where citizens are selected by lottery, allowing them to come up with proposals when parliament is trapped in gridlock.[135] Both proposals are in line with the theme that there may be better ideas and solutions out there that are not getting past the legislature.

All of these proposals, therefore, are also implicitly calling time on the idea that the representative model can be improved any further by simply "getting out the vote". We already have the evidence from democracies where voting is compulsory that the cause of the people's unhappiness with the system is not a low voter-turnout, but what the representatives do once elected. In Australia, where voting is compulsory, less than five per cent of the people said they had "a great deal" of confidence in their parliament. Eighteen per cent said "none at all" and fifty-two per cent said "not very much".[136] In Belgium, another country where voting is compulsory, more than half of the people say they "tend not to trust" their parliament.[137] In Brazil, where voting is also compulsory, over eighty per cent of Brazilians surveyed said that they were dissatisfied with the functioning of their democracy.[138] The issue is not how many people vote, therefore; it is what the representatives do with that mandate. This is a bit like the analogy of spectators at a football match. The crowd can shout advice or show their displeasure from the sidelines, but they're not the ones making the decisions during the game. The game is not designed for the players to take instructions from the crowd.

All the aforementioned ideas about how to update the representative system are still on the drawing board – they don't work in reality in any country. Our best model of a system that actually does work in a real state that contains some of these hybrid features, and from which we can learn something, is what exists in Switzerland. That country has the highest levels of trust among its citizens of any country in Europe.[139] From this we could conclude that if the Swiss people had maximum power to "update" their political system today, it is unlikely that they would radically redesign their set-up. Switzerland thus provides us with something of a social laboratory to see why this high level of trust exists there and what we might be able to learn from it for the upcoming changes in the digital age.

The Swiss system, introduced in 1848, is a functioning hybrid model that acts and feels like a typical parliamentary system, until someone flicks the switch and it temporarily morphs into a direct democracy. At that point, the legislators take a back seat, the people decide, and once the people have decided, they go back to their daily business and the legislators go back to theirs. If we come back to our football game analogy, the current Swiss model is akin to asking the players (the legislators) to get off the field and allow the spectators onto the field. The spectators decide the modifications to the rules, leave the field, and the players return to continue the game. Needless to say, logistically this all sounds terribly cumbersome, and it is. But it has worked. If it worked without a digital voting device in the past, it should work even better in the digital era when the spectators no longer need to get onto the field – they can just decide the rules from the sidelines. Secure voting technology available from mobile devices should revolutionize the representative system.

Of course, the immediate counter-argument will be that this can only work in Switzerland because it is a small, fairy-tale land high in the Alps, where there has only been brotherly love and peace for 500 years, to quote Orson Welles from the 1949 movie *The Third Man*. How could similar power-sharing arrangements possibly work in big countries with large, diverse populations?

It is true that each country is the result of its history, that no two countries are exactly alike, therefore, and that it might not be possible or even desirable to cut and paste every single aspect from the Swiss experiment. But, given what the global data is telling us about the increase in popular initiatives, referendums and electronic chatter from the unhappy masses, it may nevertheless be worth studying as we look for new political models in the digital age.

The first thing to know about Switzerland is that the Orson Wells quotes are wrong. It is what some today might call "fake news". The cuckoo clock was not invented in Switzerland and the country has a violent history.

Switzerland is divided by four official languages, three of which are shared with neighbouring countries. The territory could, therefore, have been split up among its neighbours, and that almost happened on numerous occasions, and again in 1815. In those days, the country was characterized by civil strife. Given their own rivalries, the European powers came to the conclusion that it was best for them that Switzerland should not be divided up. Eight powers, including Austria, France, Great Britain, Prussia and Russia, signed a protocol in Vienna in 1815 declaring that "the general interest demands" that Switzerland "shall enjoy perpetual neutrality".[140] Thus, neutrality was forced upon the Swiss by powerful outsiders – it was not something they inherently had or chose. The Swiss were also told to end their civil war and were given instructions on how to do it: "the Powers desire that a general amnesty be granted to all individuals led astray at a period of uncertainty and irritation" and highlighted "the necessity of mutually obliterating the remembrance of those differences which have divided them."[141]

The Swiss were not so easily tamed, though. In 1819 it looked as if they would ignore that silly notion of neutrality when a partial mobilization took place to go to war with Germany. One of the issues was that the Swiss were upset with the German state of Baden, because the Germans did not want to fix and pay for a broken bridge linking the two neighbours.[142] It did not come to war between the two states, but the Swiss have a long history of war and preparation for war. Anyone visiting the Swiss city of Basel, which borders Germany and France, might wonder why the railway station is far from the old town. That is because the Swiss thought foreign soldiers could invade Basel using that railway line.

After the 1815 Treaty of Vienna, it took one more Swiss civil war to finally draw a line behind the larger episodes of domestic violence. But it is clear from history that the Swiss do not have a "neutrality gene" or an "anti-violence gene" that only entitles them to run a high trust democracy model. They used to earn their money from mercenary work – their soldiers still protect the pope – and like in all societies, the triggers for disagreement and violence are ever-present. Over 130 incidents of "terrorism", resulting in the deaths of sixty people, have been recorded in Switzerland from 1898 to 2013.[143] On 27 September 2001, a Swiss man walked into the cantonal parliament of Zug, fired off ninety-one shots and left fourteen politicians dead. He had been angered when he received notice that he was going to be charged for arguing with a bus driver. In 2015, 333 Swiss men were not accepted for the compulsory militia because they were thought to be "too dangerous".[144]

Clearly, the problems that have plagued humankind since the days of Adam and Eve are also to be found in Switzerland. To try and counteract the people's fallen nature, and make the political system work like a Swiss clock, three tight springs are used: constrain the power of the executive, constrain the power of the legislature and constrain the power of the judiciary.

The essence of the Swiss system is that political power rests with the people, both in letter and in spirit. To reinforce this point symbolically, the country has no head of state or prime minister. There is an official who bears the title "President of the Swiss Confederation". But that person is not elected by the people and is not the head of state. The Swiss constitution tries its best to downplay the function: It is mentioned in Article 176, way below responsibility for "Water" (Article 76) and "Forestry" (Article 77).

The average Swiss does not know much about this function either. Asking the proverbial man-in-the-street who "the President" is, will usually elicit a smile, as though one is asking a trick question. But then they will put on their thinking caps and hazard a guess. Usually, the answer will be wrong.

Here, then, is a first important takeaway from the Swiss system: The system goes to great lengths to constrain the power, privilege, status and authority of the people's representatives. Accordingly, many mechanisms are put in place to prevent individual representatives from gaining too much influence.

Instead of one person at the top, the executive authority consists of a cabinet of seven councillors. Each councillor gets a turn, once every seven years, for one year only, to have the additional title of "President of the Swiss Confederation" conferred on them by parliament. Parliament tends to confer the title on the basis of a seniority principle: those who joined the cabinet last tend to have to wait their turn, which could take up to six years. It is almost as anti-strongman as the ancient Athenian system of drawing a leader by lots.

The power of the executive at the federal level is further constrained by the restriction, in place since 1850, that there can only be a maximum of seven cabinet ministers. No matter how often the cabinet members complain that they are over-worked, and that the population size has increased substantially since 1850, that constitutional restriction has not changed. Seven represented one third of the global average of twenty-two cabinet ministers per country in 2015.[145] By having a constitutional requirement that there can only be a very small number of cabinet ministers, two helpful effects are created: First, it sharply curtails the ability of the government to expand at the executive level – so costs (and taxes) tend to stay lower. Secondly, it makes for smaller, more efficient government at the top – you only have six other peers.

Moving from the executive to the legislature, the lawmakers' power is severely constrained by the people's ability to overrule and bypass their parliament. This can be done by changing the constitution without parliament's consent or by rejecting parliamentary bills. There are several ways in which legislation can be passed, but in its most extreme form, 100,000 citizens, equivalent to two per cent of the electorate of 5.1 million (in a country of 8 million), can trigger a nation-wide popular initiative that then becomes a constitutional amendment.

In this process, the legislature's role is reduced to a box-ticking, administrative function to check that the question is not about introducing a crime against humanity, that it relates to one subject per question (i.e. that it does not link several topics in a question so broad that no-one knows what the vote is about), and that it is clear from the text that accompanies the initiative question what precisely the new constitutional article is, what it strikes out, and where it would appear in the constitution. A private law firm could do these checks too, but parliament does it and then schedules the vote. Parliament's ability to delay the process is limited.[146]

The people, and not their rulers or representatives, are able to initiate a vote independently of what the legislature is doing. The initiators, therefore, decide on the timing of the vote. This has the big advantage, from the perspective of increasing trust in the system, by escalating issues early in the process. If parliament senses that the issue has the potential to cause trouble, it could try and pre-empt it by addressing the concerns it raises.

The initiators of the vote are the ones who formulate the question. Sometimes the questions are politically incorrect and even poorly phrased from a technical point of view, but that is because they have not been sanitized by a ministry for political correctness and re-written in bureaucratese.

The politically incorrect questions that non-mainstream groups pose need to be heard because, like the old expression that "a stitch in time saves nine", a problem can grow and become a big issue at the most inconvenient time.

The issue to be voted on can relate to any constitutional or legislative change that lies within the country's sovereign power. That basically means that any question that parliament can address can also be addressed by a people's initiative.[147]

Parliament is further restricted in that its own bills, drawn up by the representatives, can be subjected to a countrywide referendum if just 50,000 signatures are collected.[148] If the people object to any bill, it gets shredded. Given that there is always the risk that the people can intervene and over-rule it, this feature introduces a strong degree of external control over parliament by the people. Last, but not least, the power of the judiciary is constrained in that Swiss courts have limited power to invalidate a constitutional amendment created by an initiative, unlike in the State of California where the courts can intervene and frustrate the people's will. The only sure way to change the outcome of a popular vote is via another popular vote.[149]

Unlike the US Supreme Court, whose judges are relatively well known, the judges who serve on the Swiss Federal Supreme Court are generally not very prominent public figures. It would be a rare Swiss citizen who could name any judge serving on the country's highest court. A similar shift in power away from the judges to the people would happen in the US if the American people were able to amend their constitution by popular initiative. Rather than waiting for the judges to resolve an issue, the people would simply provide the answer directly via a constitutional amendment – and with a mobile device that would happen quickly.

Given the high level of trust and the proven stability that is associated with this particular model, it is an attractive model for the digital age.

Transposing it elsewhere, will not be easy, though. The first hurdle is that there is deep unease about giving the people too much power. These worries have a long history. Aristotle summarized the dilemma as follows: a country that doesn't allow its mass of poor people to exercise political power is eventually an unstable country, while a country that does allow its mass of poor people to exercise political power also ends up unsafe. What is one to do, then?

America's founding fathers struggled with this concept. They, too, feared rule by those without education or property. From the notes and transcriptions of the discussions at their convention of 1787, where they drafted the US constitution, we read that Alexander Hamilton, who went on to become the first US Treasury Secretary, wrote this comment in his notes at the convention: "Gentlemen say we need to be rescued from the democracy. But what the means proposed?" Hamilton's answer: "British constitution best form".[150] Hamilton was fortunate that his views were not tweeted out of the convention, coming so soon after their war of independence against the British monarch.

Another delegate quotes Hamilton saying: "See the excellency of the British executive. He can have no distinct interests from the public welfare."[151] The founding fathers harboured these fears of democracy, despite the heavy restrictions in place at the time on the ability of "the people" to vote: the electorate consisted mainly of white, free, property-owning men. Moreover, the people could not vote directly for the president, but indirectly via representatives from their respective state.

This same fear of "the masses" is why, even today, the US president is not elected directly by the people. Had that been the case, Al Gore would have won in 2000 and Hillary Clinton in 2016. Switching to a system where the American people could directly elect their president is too scary a thought, even in modern-day America.

A related argument often raised against granting the people more power is that "the masses" can be swayed by demagogues and false promises – the argument made by Plato 2,400 years ago. This fear is even greater in the internet age where the people can get their news from all kinds of (fake) sources. Even in Switzerland, with its long history of popular initiatives, there are often doubts as to whether the people will decide "wisely" when it comes to important and contentious issues. One never knows, of course, and everyone has their example of when a vote turned out to be "wrong". Yet, looking back at the outcome of many initiatives in Switzerland, one can draw the conclusion that, by and large, the people tend to vote conservatively – that is, they tend to vote to maintain the status quo, unless they think that the alternative is clearly going to be much better. Since 1848, Swiss voters have voted "no" to 89 per cent of popular initiatives.[152] It is generally hard to convince the people to freely vote for radical lurches in policies. And when, on those rare occasions, the people do vote for radical change, it is usually for one whose time has come and the writing had been on the wall long before the vote. As long as the people retain the ability to freely vote again, i.e. they do not vote to become a dictatorship, they will have the freedom to make new decisions, including correcting "mistakes".

The way the Swiss system adds an additional layer of control to try and mitigate the risk that highly controversial initiatives that get a majority of votes become law, is via a system of "double majorities". For an initiative to pass, it needs to get a majority of both the number of votes cast nationally as well as in a majority of cantons. Had the 2016 UK Brexit referendum been run as an initiative on the Swiss model, it would not have passed. The UK referendum would have required a majority of votes nationally, which it got, as well as majorities in Scotland and/or Northern Ireland, which were not obtained, in order to override the "leave" results of England and Wales. According to the

Swiss model, then, the UK "leave" vote would have failed. The "remain" campaign would have won and the Brexiteers would have had to try again another day. This shows that it is possible to have a high degree of people power, while also ensuring a high degree of checks and balances that take minority preferences into account.

Another argument against giving people too much decision-making power is the hypothesis that the people simply know too little to make informed decisions. How can "ordinary people" decide on complex issues that require a lot of time to read the documentation and understand the issues? While this is a powerful argument at first glance, its validity is undermined by the evidence that the "professionals" – our representatives – and their advisors and experts, are themselves struggling to cope.

Discussing their book *Crisis Point* (2016), two former US senators, Trent Lott and Tom Daschle, pointed out that members of Congress fly out of Washington on Thursdays, return on Tuesdays, and effectively only have Wednesdays to work. This means, Senator Daschle said, that "you won't have the time you need to do the governance part of the job like you're supposed to."[153] This is not a US issue only. The reform package passed by the Greek parliament in May 2016 contained 7,500 pages. No representative could have read that, or known its full implications, yet they voted it into law.

Not reading or understanding the text one votes into law has consequences. There are cases where legislation containing serious technical mistakes has been passed into law by the professionals. In 2004, lawmakers in the State of Virginia accidentally outlawed all exemptions for working on Sundays.[154] That mistake was overlooked by several four-eyes checks, including by the legal staff of the legislature and by the governor, who signed it into law. The mistake was found by a member of the public, after the law was already in force. Our representatives are signing bills that they don't always read and don't always fully understand.

A further argument against giving the people more power in a democracy is that "the masses" can act too emotionally and irrationally. They are accused of never voting on the actual question, but on some other gripe that is not on the ballot and, therefore, they often get the answer "wrong". This argument, too, is undermined by the voting behaviour of the experts. If one considers that the clever, well-educated and rational people who sit on the US Supreme Court delivered split rulings based *on the exact same facts* fifty-four per cent of the time from 2008 to 2015,[155] then why should ordinary voters not be permitted to disagree on the importance they want to attach to the facts they hear about?

We have also seen little evidence of the supposed careful weighing of the pros and cons of arguments that was supposed to come from informed debate among the professional rulers of nations. Consider the case of the First World War, which caused over 17 million deaths. Even today, more than a century after that war, with so many books having analysed those events, there are still competing narratives as to what exactly triggered that catastrophe. What the archives do show, however, is that no representative in their wildest dreams had expected it to turn out that badly for their side. There were obviously some monumental miscalculations, which ultimately led, inter alia, to the Second World War, seven decades of communism in Russia, and Britain losing its Empire.

The decision to send an army to war is almost always taken by just a few individuals. It would be very difficult to get an entire electorate to support an offensive first strike when the threat to the nation is not obvious.

The March 2003 invasion of Iraq was supposedly predicated on intelligence information that Saddam Hussein had weapons of mass destruction. In January 2003, more than sixty per cent of Americans wanted President Bush to find a diplomatic solution, seventy-seven per cent wanted to see hard evidence that the weapons existed, and if they were not found, they wanted the international community to keep looking. Fifty-five per cent thought that President Bush was too quick to involve the military option and sixty-two per cent thought that US involvement in Iraq would increase terrorism.[156] That was a poll of the American people *before the war*. With the benefit of hindsight, a decade and a half later, it appears that "the ordinary people" were instinctively more careful about the pros and cons of that particular war than "the professionals" had been with all their advisors. That war, it now turns out, was based on "fake news". The ordinary people did not buy it – the small group of professionals did.

Another example of how the professionals are not always sufficiently carefully weighing the pros and cons that their actions can have, comes to us from the 2016 UK referendum on whether or not to remain in the EU. With the benefit of perfect hindsight, given how important the issue of immigration had apparently become, we can now say that the UK professionals had been wrong not to have opted for the immigration restrictions that were legally available to all EU member states when 75 million people from eastern Europe joined the EU in 2004. EU law at that time permitted immigration restrictions of *up to seven years* from 2004 (Spain chose two, France four, Germany seven, and Switzerland, which is not a member of the EU but has access via bilateral deals, effectively got ten). The Swiss negotiators knew that their EU deal would subsequently have to be approved by the people in a referendum. The UK negotiators, who thought they had zero referendum risk, opted for zero. Merely knowing that the people have the power to over-rule what the professionals have negotiated on the people's behalf, would produce a far greater degree of alignment between the people and their representatives. In the years before the 2004 accession of the new states to the EU, surveys in the UK in 1999, 2001 and 2003 consistently showed that *two-thirds* of British residents were against an immigration policy that was decided jointly with the EU.[157] Needless to say, the British representatives are merely human and cannot always know what the people want, but that is where the people's direct involvement would quickly clarify things. If the British people had had the power to launch their "worried about immigration" initiative before 2004, this little topic would have been addressed early on.

Then there is the argument against giving the people more direct power that comes from the bad experiences from those jurisdictions where direct democracy already exists in one form or another. Here we get to hear about all the things that can go wrong: campaigns can be launched by special interests with a lot of money behind them; some of these special interests try to game the system by launching initiatives that polarize and spill over to the general elections; the voters don't always understand the questions on the ballot or the financial implications of their decisions; it can lead to contradictory policies and new forms of gridlock and uncertainty. In short, direct democracy is characterized as worse than the representative system. The problem with this line of reasoning is that the people in those jurisdictions disagree. Even if people are aware of these real-life problems, solid majorities continue to support direct democracy – even in the State of California, where these problems have received quite a bit of coverage.[158] If direct democracy were so bad, the people would voluntarily have handed power back to their representatives. That has not happened anywhere. On the contrary, the evidence globally is that we are moving to more direct democracy, not less, precisely because the representative system has bigger weaknesses.

Given that we're *de facto* already in a proto-type hybrid model in more places, it appears that it's inevitable that the *de jure* part will follow. In the weakest form of this upgrade, which is available in the UK (since 2011) and Finland (since 2012), the people can initiate an online petition for an act that *might* be debated in parliament if it reaches a certain number of signatures (100,000 in the UK, 50,000 in Finland). In that model, power is still firmly in the representatives' hands, but the people can influence the agenda, let off steam and perhaps force a debate on an issue they think is pressing.

In its most extreme form, which exists in Switzerland, the people can write their constitutional amendment directly and it can become the law of the land without the legislature or the courts able to stop it. The Swiss do not typically bother with petitions, therefore.

Technology is making it easier to collect signatures and launch initiatives. The consequence of this could be huge. Safeguards built into constitutions before anyone considered the impact of internet voting, could suddenly become unlocked. Article 11 of the European Union's Lisbon Treaty (2007) says that "one million citizens who are nationals of a significant number of Member States" can launch an initiative "inviting" (but not ordering) the European Commission to draft a new law where the people think it is required. Perhaps one million was a big, paper-based hurdle in 2007, but not any more. The day may come when the people's "invitation" becomes difficult to ignore.

It appears likely, therefore, that over time, the ability to ping the legislature via the internet (e.g. in the form of the good old petition, say) will lead to more issues being raised by the public and that one of those issues may well end up being a petition for greater power for the people. The "danger" (some would say "opportunity") with today's online petitions, therefore, is that they open the possibility to a form of government that dare not speak its name – direct people power in more places, at more levels of government and in connection with more issues.

As the shift towards a hybrid system appears to be on the way in more places, it will attract more attention as a potential model in the West as well as in the East. The world's most populous country, China, will inevitably have to consider the advantages and disadvantages of that model too, as the country continues to reform politically. Experiments are under way with competitive elections in some of China's villages, home to some six hundred million people in rural areas. [159] The attractions of a hybrid model "with Chinese characteristics", no doubt, are likely to include its inherent conservatism, i.e. the difficulty in getting the people, especially an ageing population, to vote for revolutionary policy lurches. A greater degree of direct democracy at local and provincial levels would also act as a check on the power of a strongman in local and regional fiefdoms. Thanks to mobile voting devices, direct democracy at the level of the central government would logistically be easier than ever before, which means that "stabilisers" would need to be built in. One such stabilizer could be the use of the Swiss "double majority" principle: a popular initiative requires a majority of both voters as well as a majority of the regions. That mechanism would reduce the possibility that one populous part of the country would consistently get its way. Another stabilizer could be a high voting threshold: a high proportion of voters would be required to launch initiatives and to get them approved (above twenty-five per cent of the electorate, say; perhaps even as high as fifty per cent). That way, only the really important issues about which the overwhelming majority of people feel strongly, would stand a chance of being decided directly by the people. An additional characteristic of the hybrid model that would be attractive to China is that it tends to turn the representatives into implementers of settled popular will. To illustrate what this means, we can take the example of the British prime minister's resignation after he lost the Brexit referendum. He took the people's decision as also having consequences for him. In contrast, no Swiss cabinet minister would dream of resigning when the people reject their recommendations, which they often do. The Swiss version of the hybrid model assumes that the people are there to tell the representatives what they want, and it is the job of the representatives to implement that decision. The idea that China's representatives could stay in office after losing a referendum might appeal to many in a country with a long meritocratic tradition when it comes to the professional class managing the affairs of state.

While China's adoption of a hybrid system "with Chinese characteristics" would be a game changer for China and the world, the most likely place where we could see faster progress in the transition to such an arrangement is likely to be Europe. That continent is heaving with a wide variety of political models, from kingdoms and principalities to republics, some with strong degrees of direct democracy and some with little. Several of these countries are members of overlapping unions and alliances where sovereignty has been pooled on issues as central to statehood as the currency and defence. This region is open to a lot of experimentation when it comes to giving the people more power.

We won't know what too much freedom is in the digital age until it has been tried somewhere and shown to have failed spectacularly. But even then, we would need to understand the context of that failure. Not being an innovator, though, and simply waiting to see how technology transforms democracy in other places, is also a strategy for a while. But leaving the representative model from the late 1700s unreformed indefinitely is not – nowhere.

CONCLUDING THOUGHTS

DRIVERS AND SCENARIOS

Three hundred years ago there were fewer choices to be made. People had less, knew less and tolerated more. The slaves did their long hours of work and the women were voteless. Today, women can vote, the slaves have been freed and the variety of interests and preferences in civil society are so many and so diverse, that it is not possible for a single party to adequately reflect them all. This inability of the representative system to adequately reflect more of the issues that are relevant for an increasingly differentiated population is obviously going to become even more difficult as diversity increases still further. That mattered less when the government was tiny and offered little on its product shelf. But, today that government product shelf is vast and the role of government pervasive. In the decades ahead, the role of the state will grow further as it expands into new areas and as the long-predicted demographic trends become more apparent in more places. To argue the opposite, namely, that the role of the state will decline in the decades ahead, requires a spreadsheet that shows the reversal of the demographic trend of an ageing population, lower government expenditure for social security, pensions and healthcare, a long series of budget surpluses to start paying back debt, a trend towards lower taxes, year after year, the shift towards less and less regulation, and higher economic growth than we've had over the previous half century. We could throw in a few other positive assumptions into that spreadsheet, such as the discovery of cheap, clean, limitless energy, and robots doing the work so that the people can live a life of leisure. Such a blue-sky scenario is not impossible, of course, but it does not seem very realistic at the moment. The realistic and reasonable variables in our spreadsheet point, therefore, to an unreformed representative system going to face even bigger challenges to please the unhappy crowds in the decades ahead.

Our starting point is a representative model that is unpopular and, for the first time in history, technology is opening up the possibility for a new arrangement for the people to express their will. Three hundred years ago, it was thought that the best way to distil the people's will was via a layer of wise representatives. Today, technology is creating the possibility to redesign that interaction.

The shift towards a more digital form of interaction between citizens and their government is being driven by five main forces:

First, democracy is not a static thing. As Plato pointed out 2,400 years ago, democracy has a tendency to hand out more and more rights and freedoms. What we are experiencing today is not the same democracy that our grandparents knew. Citizens are deciding directly on more things more often, as shown by the surge of petitions, initiatives and referendums across the globe. Technology is accelerating this trend. The ubiquitous nature of hand-held devices for sending and receiving messages about anything and everything, is further shifting power to the holders of those devices.

The second driver for more digital interaction between citizens and their representatives ironically comes from the representatives themselves. Their primary motivation is to offer their citizens "convenience" and "participation". Instead of having to stand in queues, citizens will be able to vote from home or from their mobile devices. Their objective is also to make it easier to "get out the vote" (especially if it means voting for them or their party). Who can be against that? Well, many it seems. Since no legislator will vote for laws that are likely to boost the opposition's chances at the polls, no government agency will have the money to test an internet-based voting system unless the legislature grants the necessary funding. At times, when the proponents of a digital transformation are in power, big strides will be made towards rolling it out. The moment the opponents get the upper hand in the legislature, though, funding will be cut off. In each and every electoral jurisdiction, the different political parties are going to draw their own conclusions about how good such a digital transformation is going to be for their own electoral prospects. There will, no doubt, be many interesting case studies from all over the world highlighting the activities by the supporters and opponents of this new voting technology. Always and everywhere, there will be more that divides the proponents and opponents of internet voting than the issue of cybersecurity alone. This battle will be fought out again and again, jurisdiction by jurisdiction, but the war will eventually be won by those providing an acceptable technological solution. Where technology leads, society and the law eventually follow.

The third driver for this new style of digital interaction is the IT industry, which is designing out-of-the-box software and hardware solutions to run elections via digital means. These vendor solutions are getting better and better at ensuring that elections held via the internet are verifiably safer and more accurate than plain paper-based systems. Their business is to develop the software and hardware that governments can use to receive secure instructions from their citizens. The IT industry is not going to stop trying to perfect this arrangement.

The fourth driver in favour of this new technology comes from a disparate range of non-governmental forces: from "the grassroots", "civic society", idealists, visionaries and revolutionaries from the left, the centre and the right. They want to "improve" the representative model. They're not in agreement about what the new model should look like, but they are intrigued by the idea that the digital age is opening up new possibilities for citizens to participate even more in the democratic process. This driver is underestimated as a potential for disruption. Much of what is happening at the local level goes unreported nationally and internationally, despite the universal experience that "all politics is local". By the time the ruling elite discovers what the people "out there" really want, it's very late in the day.

The fifth driving force for a digital shift is to be found among the general public, who are currently not too focused on this topic. Every now and again, when the issue of internet voting is raised, ordinary people wonder why it is possible to do e-banking by internet, but not to vote by internet. Over time this curiosity in the topic could result in a more meaningful driving force for change. As the government begins to offer more and more services online that will require higher levels of cybersecurity, more and more people are likely to notice that almost all dealings with the government have shifted online, except the really important one of instructing the people's representatives. Some people may eventually ask the question why this is the case.

Taken together, these five driving forces: the tendency for democracy to try to become more representative, the top-down political forces that want to deliver more "convenience" to the voters, the IT vendors who earn their living from rolling out better software on which to run elections, the bottom-up idealists, and ordinary members of the public who are ready to try out something new with their mobile devices, will propel us further in the direction of a greater use of information technology in the democratic process.

What will the consequences of such a shift be? Where might that lead?

In a base case assumption, more rights for citizens in the more transparent digital age leads to improved governance and better outcomes. The evidence presented in this book supports the case that, by and large, over a period of many centuries, the people can be trusted with more decision-making power. As long as the people do not vote to turn their country into a dictatorship, they will have the chance to vote again and modify or overturn the decisions they no longer like.

There is also a less optimistic scenario, however, akin to Plato's forecast that "tyranny naturally derives out of democracy". Under certain circumstances, people might vote for the demagogue's proposals, which eventually lead them down the wrong path.

In the digital age, the risks are compounded by an overload of information. Instead of the internet inaugurating the golden age of an informed citizenry, where everyone has access to the truth at their fingertips, there are now many courts of public opinion, each with its own facts. In such an environment, a digital form of democracy, in which citizens have an electronic ballot in their pocket, could be a more volatile arrangement. It is not that the facts are not available on the internet. Even when we do have the facts, we might not attach the same weight to their significance as others do. That was always the case. That's the essence of freedom, after all. Plato wrote that a democracy is a place where "a man may say and do what he likes." Demagogues, who

Plato warned are democracy's undoing, should find a breeding ground in such a scenario. This less optimistic scenario will probably materialize in some places in the digital age, just as it has in previous ages for other reasons. The way to try and mitigate that risk is by making it difficult for the demagogue to bypass the people. Every important decision needs to come before the people. Even better would be the arrangement to permit the people to launch their own initiatives in competition to those of the demagogue. Let the best ideas compete.

For our pessimistic scenario, we have to recognize that despite the best intentions of the framers of smart constitutions, there is no mechanism that can provide an absolute guarantee that a tyrant can't come to power ever. The most we can do is to make it very difficult.

The pessimistic scenario is not the base case scenario of this book. The base case scenario of this book is that seeking refuge in an unreformed representative system from the late 1700s is the real danger. An unreformed representative system from the late 1700s is not going to survive the disruption of the digital era.

Notes

[1] Krimmer, Robert. 2012. *The Evolution of E-voting: Why Voting Technology is Used and How It Affects Democracy,* Tallinn University of Technology Doctoral Theses Series I: Social Sciences, No. 19, Tut Press, pp. 16-17.

[2] United States Election Assistance Commission, "Testing and Certification Technical Paper #2: A Survey of Internet Voting", http://www.eac.gov/assets/1/Documents/SIV-FINAL.pdf; Goodman, Nicole and Smith, Rodney. 2016. *Internet Voting in Sub-National Elections: Policy Learning in Canada and Australia,* paper presented at the International Conference on Electronic Voting, "E-Vote-ID 2016", 18–21 October 2016, Lochau/Bregenz, Austria; Goodman, Nicole J. & Pammett, Jon H. "The Patchwork of Internet Voting in Canada", http://www.e-voting.cc/wp-content/uploads/downloads/2014/10/evote2014_goodmann_pammett_p13-18.pdf; Government of New Zealand, Department of Internal Affairs, "Online Voting", http://www.dia.govt.nz/online-voting

[3] All data related to Estonian elections comes from the Estonian National Election Committee, http://www.vvk.ee/voting-methods-in-estonia/engindex/statistics. The availability of the i-ballot has contributed to an increased voter turnout in parliamentary elections in Estonia from 58.2 per cent in 2003, before this option was introduced, to 61.9 per cent in 2007, 63.5 per cent in 2011 and to 64.2 per cent in 2015. The number of i-ballots cast from abroad increased from 2 per cent in 2007 (from 51 countries), to 3.9 per cent in 2011 (from 105 countries) to 5.7 per cent in 2015 (from 116 countries). The share of i-ballots of the total turnout rose from 1.9 per cent in 2005 to 24.3 per cent in 2011 and 30.5 per cent in 2015. The percentage of i-ballots using mobile phones as part of the identification process increased from 1.9 per cent in 2011 to 12.2 per cent in 2015. The Estonians have used the i-ballot in eight elections so far: In local elections in October 2005, October 2009 and October 2013, in parliamentary elections in March 2007, March 2011 and March 2015, and in elections for the European Parliament in June 2009 and May 2014.

[4] Luechinger, Simon et al. July 2006. "The Impact of Postal Voting on Participation: Evidence for Switzerland", Working Paper No. 297, Institute for Empirical Research in Economics, University of Zurich, http://www.econ.uzh.ch/static/wp_iew/iewwp297.pdf.

[5] Barrat, Jordi. 2015. "The French Conseil Constitutionnel and Electronic Voting", in Driza Mauer, Ardita & Barrat, Jordi (eds.), *E-Voting Case Law: A Comparative Analysis.* Ashgate Publishing Ltd.

[6] Sénat (France). Session Ordinaire de 2013-2014, Enregistré à la Présidence du Sénat, No. 445, 9 April 2014, p. 37.

[7] ibid.

[8] Garriaud-Maylam, Joëlle, "Le vote Internet fait flop", 22 May 2014, http://www.joellegarriaud.com/2014/05/le-vote-internet-fait-flop/

[9] An early adopter of internet voting has been the Canton of Geneva, which during the test phase rolled out the i-ballot to its citizens resident abroad. The share of the canton's eligible citizens residing abroad who opted to use the i-ballot instead of a postal vote increased from thirty per cent of that group's votes in 2010 to forty-eight per cent by 2014. The share of those aged 18-29 using this approach increased from forty-seven per cent to sixty-one per cent, and for those aged sixty and above, usage increased from twenty-five per cent to thirty-seven per cent. Source: Canton of Geneva, http://www.ge.ch/votations/. Since each canton slices and dices its statistics differently, data from the Canton of Neuchâtel shows that the i-ballot was used by two per cent of those aged ninety-five years and above in a February 2016 poll. Canton of Neuchâtel, http://www.ne.ch/autorites/CHAN/elections-votations/stat/Stat/Scrutin_20160228/evo_TT_mode_global.pdf

[10] United Kingdom Parliament. *Report of the Speaker's Commission on Digital Democracy*, 26 Jan 2015, http://digitaldemocracy.parliament.uk/documents/Open-Up-Digital-Democracy-Report.pdf

[11] ibid.

[12] A review of studies on who used the internet to vote in specific cases in Estonia, Switzerland, Norway, the United Kingdom, the United States and Canada, found that the voters tended to be younger than the non-internet voters, but they were not the youngest category of voters. This suggested that internet voting was unlikely to draw out younger voters who currently tend to stay away from the polls, simply because the voting mechanism had changed from paper to an electronic device. See

Serdült, Uwe, et al. "Who are the Internet Voters?" in Tambouris, E. et al. (eds.) 2015. *Electronic Government and Electronic Participation.*

[13] Hapsara, Manik et al. 2016. *E-voting in Developing Countries: Current Landscapes and Future Research Agenda,* Paper presented at the International Conference on Electronic Voting, "E-Vote-ID 2016", 18–21 October 2016, Lochau/Bregenz, Austria.

[14] Arizona Secretary of State. "Military and Overseas Voters", http://www.azsos.gov/elections/voting-election/military-and-overseas-voters; United States Election Assistance Commission, "Projects to Support Military and Overseas Voters/UOCAVA Remote Electronic Absentee Voting Pilot Project", http://www.eac.gov/testing_and_certification/eacs_work_with_military_and_overs eas_voting.aspx; United States Election Assistance Commission, "Testing and Certification Technical Paper #2, A Survey of Internet Voting", 14 September 2011, http://www.eac.gov/assets/1/Documents/SIV-FINAL.pdf

[15] Driza Mauer, Ardita and Barrat, Jordi (eds.). 2015. *E-Voting Case Law: A Comparative Analysis.* Routledge.

[16] Höber, Hilmar. "Ein Hauch genügt - und die Waage gibt an", *Neue Zürcher Zeitung*, 28 February 2003, http://www.nzz.ch/article8P7V0-1.219790

[17] Bull, Christian et al. 2016. "The Imperfect Storm". Paper presented at the International Conference on Electronic Voting, "E-Vote-ID 2016", 18–21 October 2016, Lochau/Bregenz, Austria.

[18] Nakashima, Ellen. 29 August 2016. "Russian hackers targeted Arizona election system", *Washington Post*, https://www.washingtonpost.com/world/national-security/fbi-is-investigating-foreign-hacks-of-state-election-systems/2016/08/29/6e758ff4-6e00-11e6-8365-b19e428a975e_story.html

[19] US Vote Foundation. "The Future of Voting. End-to-End Verifiable Internet Voting Specification and Feasibility Assessment Study", July 2015, https://www.usvotefoundation.org/sites/default/files/E2EVIV_full_report.pdf

[20] A survey by the University of New South Wales in Canberra, Australia, of academic papers on the i-ballot in developing countries, found that the research focused mainly on the technological aspects – as though all a government had to do was simply install the software and then run the election over the internet. Hapsara,

Manik et al. 2016. *E-voting in Developing Countries: Current Landscapes and Future Research Agenda,* Paper presented at the International Conference on Electronic Voting, "E-Vote-ID 2016", 18–21 October 2016, Lochau/Bregenz, Austria.

[21] Bull, Christian et al. 2016, "The Imperfect Storm", Paper presented at the International Conference on Electronic Voting, "E-Vote-ID 2016", 18–21 October 2016, Lochau/Bregenz, Austria.

[22] Rothman, Lily, 19 October 2016, "Has an Election Ever Been Rigged in U.S. History?", *Time*, http://time.com/4536566/rigged-election-american-history

[23] Greenberg, David. 16 October 2000. "Was Nixon Robbed?", *Slate*, http://www.slate.com/articles/news_and_politics/history_lesson/2000/10/was_nixon_robbed.html

[24] Johnson, Jenna. 18 October 2016. "Donald Trump says the election is 'rigged'", *Washington Post*, https://www.washingtonpost.com/news/post-politics/wp/2016/10/18/donald-trump-says-the-election-is-rigged-heres-what-his-supporters-think-that-means/?utm_term=.886c7c15c7e9

[25] http://www.usatoday.com/story/news/politics/2017/01/25/donald-trump-voter-fraud-charles-schumer-elijah-cummings/97030320/

[26] Bremmer, Dale, 2003. "The Outcome of the 2000 Florida Presidential Election: An Econometric Postmortem", https://www.rose-hulman.edu/~bremmer/professional/florida_election_ballot.pdf

[27] Bailey, Rishab & Sharma, Rohit. 2015. "E-Voting Case Law in India", in Driza Mauer, Ardita & Barrat, Jordi (eds.), *E-Voting Case Law: A Comparative Analysis*. Ashgate Publishing Ltd., p. 101.

[28] Saxena, Anupam. 23 March 2011. "Gujarat Implements e-Voting For Municipal Elections; 1582 e-Voters Register", http://www.medianama.com/2011/03/223-gujarat-implements-e-voting-for-municipal-elections-1582-e-voters-register/

[29] "Internet access is a 'fundamental right'", 8 March 2010, BBC, http://news.bbc.co.uk/2/hi/technology/8548190.stm

[30] United Nations' Human Rights Council, Thirty-Second Session, Agenda Item 3, 27 June 2016, https://www.article19.org/data/files/Internet_Statement_Adopted.pdf

[31] Judgment in Case C-131/12 Google Spain SL, Google Inc. v Agencia Española de Protección de Datos, Mario Costeja González, Press Release No. 70/14, Luxembourg, 13 May 2014, http://curia.europa.eu/jcms/upload/docs/application/pdf/2014-05/cp140070en.pdf

[32] Article 31(1), "Wet van 30 september 2014, houdende regels inzake het raadgevend referendum", http://wetten.overheid.nl/BWBR0036443/2015-07-01

[33] Nijeboer, Arjen. "The Dutch Consultative Referendum Law: An Overview", https://www.meerdemocratie.nl/dutch-consultative-referendum-law-overview

[34] Ballot Act of 1872

[35] Heckelman, J.C. 1995. "The Effect of the Secret Ballot on Voter Turnout Rates", *Public Choice* (1995) 82: 107. doi:10.1007/BF01047732

[36] Yakobson, Alexander. 1995. "Secret Ballot and Its Effects in the Late Roman Republic", *Hermes*, Vol. 123, No. 4, pp. 426-442.

[37] Academic research suggests that family members share information about who they're voting for. This was also inferred from an analysis of IP log data in "Estonia Family Voting Patterns in E-vote Log Data: Estonian Electronic Elections 2013-2015" by Unt, Taavi et al., and in the recorded case of a husband voting electronically for his wife in Norway, cited in Bull, Christian et al. in "The imperfect storm". Both papers were presented at the International Conference on Electronic Voting, "E-Vote-ID 2016", 18–21 October 2016, Lochau/Bregenz, Austria.

[38] Kappeler, Beat, 27 May 2007, "Wählen ab 16? - Besser wäre ein Stimmrecht ab Geburt", *Neue Zürcher Zeitung;* Lahni, Erhard, 15 July 2008, "Wahlrecht ab Geburt", https://sites.google.com/site/familienpartei/Home/wir_ueber_uns/wahlrecht-ab-geburt; "Familienverband für "Wahlrecht ab Geburt", 16 July 2012, *Der Standard*, http://derstandard.at/1342139174773/Familienverband-fordert-Kinderstimmrecht; Ingber, Lea, 15 July 2014, "Ein Kind, eine Stimme", *Neue Zürcher Zeitung*, http://www.nzz.ch/schweiz/ein-kind-eine-stimme-1.18343423

[39] Plato, *The Republic* (translated by Benjamin Jowett), Book VIII.

[40] Rousseau, Jean-Jacques. 1762. *Du contrat social ou Principes du droit politique*, Book III, Chapter XV.

[41] Database of the Centre for Research on Direct Democracy, http://www.c2d.ch, for the period 1792-2014, with the assistance of Uwe Serdült, and country-by-country web searches for 2015 and 2016.

[42] ibid.

[43] European Union Act (2011), Section 6: "Decisions requiring approval by Act and by referendum", http://www.legislation.gov.uk/ukpga/2011/12/section/6/enacted

[44] Source for Finland and Portugal: Butler, David & Ranney, Austin (eds.). 1994. *Referendums Around the World: The Growing Use of Direct Democracy.* Macmillan.

[45] Nijeboer, Arjen. 2005. "The Dutch Referendum", in *European Constitutional Law Review*, 1: 393–405, 2005.

[46] World Values Survey, http://www.worldvaluessurvey.org

[47] "Große Mehrheit für Volksentscheide auf Bundesebene", 17 November 2013, *Focus*, http://www.focus.de/politik/deutschland/das-volk-ruft-nach-mehr-demokratie-deutliche-mehrheit-fuer-volksentscheide-auf-bundesebene-_aid_1160857.html; Support for more direct democracy among citizens in Germany is generally around eighty per cent according to Decker, Frank. 2016. *Der Irrweg der Volksgesetzgebung.* Dietz. p. 11.

[48] https://de.wikipedia.org/wiki/Liste_der_Plebiszite_in_Deutschland; From 1946 to 2015, over 300 popular initiatives have been recorded at the Länder level, according to Decker, Frank. 2016. *Der Irrweg der Volksgesetzgebung.* Dietz. p. 105.

[49] This data (8,000 initiatives at the local level and 300 at the Länder level) was attributed to Claudine Nierth in an interview with Françoise Schmid-Bechtel in *Aargauer Zeitung*, 7 December 2016.

[50] Guam, Mariana Islands, Marshall Islands, Micronesia, Nauru, New Caledonia, Niue, Palau, Tokelau and Tuvalu. Morris, Caroline. "Referendums in Oceania", in Qvortrup, Matt (ed.). 2014. *Referendums Around the World: The Continued Growth of Direct Democracy.* Palgrave Macmillan.

[51] In April 2016, the Dutch used their new right of initiative to vote "no" to a treaty between the European Union and the Ukraine. The Netherlands was the only EU country where this treaty was subjected to a referendum, and only because of this new tool. In the case of the 2,137-page long EU treaty with Ukraine, the referendum shone a light on the fact that this was more than an economic treaty – it included references to military cooperation. Given the shifting borders between Russia and Ukraine, and a strengthened NATO presence in the region, these clauses in the treaty were not without relevance. It is not clear that, had the people in the European Union been asked in April 2016 whether they wanted to deepen security cooperation with Ukraine, as stated in this treaty, that they would have agreed to that.

[52] Okamato, Mitsuhiko et al., "Direct Democracy in Japan", *C2D Working Paper Series* 47/2014, http://www.zora.uzh.ch/103334/1/C2D_WP47.pdf

[53] Van San, Shannon. "Macau Referendum Organizers Arrested", 25 August 2014, http://www.voanews.com/content/organizers-of-macau-referendum-arrested/2427149.html

[54] Singh, Soibam Rocky, 24 June 2016, "No provision for referendum in India: Experts on Kejriwal's call for Delhi vote", *Hindustan Times,* http://www.hindustantimes.com/delhi/no-provision-for-referendum-in-india-experts-on-kejriwal-s-call-for-delhi-vote/story-mMj77ofwAK55aJQlNovxRN.html.

[55] Source: Compiled from data in Donovan, Todd. "Referendums and initiatives in North America" in Qvortrup, Matt (ed.). 2014. *Referendums Around the World: The Continued Growth of Direct Democracy.* Palgrave Macmillan.

[56] Donovan, Todd. "Referendums and Initiatives in North America", in Qvortrup, Matt (ed.). 2014. *Referendums Around the World: The Continued Growth of Direct Democracy.* Palgrave Macmillan.

[57] Altic, Josh & Pallay, Geoff, 31 August 2016, "Ballot Measures: American Direct Democracy at Work", *New York Times,*

https://www.nytimes.com/2016/08/31/opinion/campaign-stops/ballot-measures-american-direct-democracy-at-work.html?_r=0

[58] National Conference of State Legislatures' Ballot Measures databases for the period from 1902 to 2015, http://www.ncsl.org

[59] Sources: For the US, National Conference of State Legislatures' Ballot Measures Database for the period from 1902 to 2016.
http://www.ncsl.org/research/elections-and-campaigns/ballot-measures-database.aspx, for the rest of the world: Centre for Research on Direct Democracy (1792-2014); web searches for 2015 and 2016.

[60] Magleby, David. "Direct Legislation in the American States" in Butler, David & Ranney, Austin 1994. *Referendums Around the World*. MacMillan.

[61] Recent referendums held in Africa include: Senegal (2001, 2016), the Ivory Coast (2016), South Sudan (2011, 2016), Zambia (2016), the Central African Republic (2004, 2015), Congo (2002, 2015), Rwanda (2003, 2015), Zimbabwe (2013), Equatorial Guinea, Liberia (2011), Kenya (2005, 2010), Madagascar (2007, 2010), Niger (2009, 2010), Comoros (2001, 2009), Mauritania (2006), Burundi, Chad, Uganda (2005), and Botswana (2001).

[62] Kersting, Norbert. "Referendums in Africa", in Qvortrup, Matt (ed.). 2014. *Referendums Around the World: The Continued Growth of Direct Democracy*. Palgrave Macmillan.

[63] www.itu.org

[64] Algeria (2005), Bahrain (2001, 2014), Egypt (2005, 2007, 2011, 2014), Iraq (2002, 2005), Morocco (2011), Qatar (2003), Syria (2000, 2007, 2012), Tunisia (2002), and Yemen (2001).

[65] Article 1 of Iran's 1979 Constitution, http://iranonline.com/iran/iran-info/Government/constitution-1.html

[66] Article 177 of the Constitution of Iran (1979).

[67] Article 59 of the Constitution of Iran (1979).

[68] "Saddam scores 100% in leadership ballot", *The Guardian*, 16 October 2002, https://www.theguardian.com/world/2002/oct/16/iraq

[69] Plato, *The Republic* (translated by Benjamin Jowett), Book VIII.

[70] Based on Wikipedia searches for "List of monarchs who lost their thrones", 14 October 2016.

[71] Sources: The data for the US comes from Gallup http://www.gallup.com/poll/1597/Confidence-Institutions.aspx and represents the trend data from 1973 to 2015. The data for all other countries comes from the World Values Survey http://www.worldvaluessurvey.org

[72] European Commission, "Eurobarometer of November 2015", http://ec.europa.eu/public_opinion/index_en.htm

[73] Gallup News Service, "June 2-7, 2015 – Final Topline", interviews conducted June 2-7, 2015, http://www.gallup.com/file/poll/183602/150615Confidence.pdf

[74] Unless stated otherwise, the data about confidence in the legislature refers to the percentage of people who had a "great deal" of confidence in their legislature, World Values Survey, http://www.worldvaluessurvey.org

[75] Plato, *The Republic* (translated by Benjamin Jowett), Book VIII.

[76] ibid.

[77] Hayek, F.A. 1944. *The Road to Serfdom.* Routledge, pp. 140-143.

[78] "What's gone wrong with democracy", *The Economist*, 1 March 2014, and "The party's (largely) over", 21 October 2010, http://www.economist.com/node/17306082

[79] Hibbing, John R. and Theiss-Morse, Elizabeth, 2 May 2016, "A surprising number of Americans dislike how messy democracy is. They like Trump", *Washington Post*, https://www.washingtonpost.com/news/monkey-cage/wp/2016/05/02/a-surprising-number-of-americans-dislike-how-messy-democracy-is-they-like-trump/

[80] "Apenas 14% dos brasileiros se dizem satisfeitos com a democracia", IBPOE, 25 April 2016, http://www.ibopeinteligencia.com/noticias-e-pesquisas/apenas-14-dos-brasileiros-se-dizem-satisfeitos-com-a-democracia/

[81] United Nations, http://csonet.org/index.php?menu=30

[82] https://parliamentfights.wordpress.com

[83] Wan, William. "In China, officials' watches get watched", *Washington Post*, https://www.washingtonpost.com/world/asia_pacific/in-china-officials-watches-get-watched/2012/09/13/4e9937f2-f8e4-11e1-8398-0327ab83ab91_story.html

[84] Clover, Charles. 10 March 2016, "China public outcry over finance minister comments", *Financial Times*, https://www.ft.com/content/c877fdc6-e67d-11e5-bc31-138df2ae9ee6

[85] "Into the abyss", 5 November 2016, *The Economist*, http://www.economist.com/news/europe/21709508-fran-ois-hollandes-approval-falls-4-abyss

[86] Frey, C.B. and Osborne, M.A. 2013. *The Future of Employment: How Susceptible are Jobs to Computerization?* University of Oxford.

[87] Arntz, M. et al. 2016. "The Risk of Automation for Jobs in OECD Countries: A Comparative Analysis", *OECD Social, Employment and Migration Working Papers*, No. 189, OECD Publishing, Paris. http://dx.doi.org/10.1787/5jlz9h56dvq7-en

[88] United Nations, Department of Economic and Social Affairs, Population Division (2015). World Population Prospects: The 2015 Revision, http://www.un.org/en/development/desa/population/

[89] Plato, *The Republic* (translated by Benjamin Jowett), Book VIII.

[90] Friedman, Milton & Friedman Rose, 1990. *Free to Choose*. Pan Books, p. 116.

[91] Plato, *The Republic* (translated by Benjamin Jowett), Book VIII.

[92] United Nations, Department of Economic and Social Affairs, Population Division (2015). *World Population Prospects: The 2015 Revision*, custom data acquired via website.

[93] United Nations, Department of Economic and Social Affairs, Population Division (2015). *World Population Prospects: The 2015 Revision*, custom data acquired via website.

[94] International Monetary Fund, *Fiscal Monitor*, April 2016, http://www.imf.org/external/pubs/ft/fm/2016/01/pdf/fm1601.pdf, Table A23, page 97.

[95] International Monetary Fund, *Fiscal Monitor*, April 2016, http://www.imf.org/external/pubs/ft/fm/2016/01/pdf/fm1601.pdf, Table A24, page 98.

[96] International Monetary Fund, *Fiscal Monitor*, April 2016, http://www.imf.org/external/pubs/ft/fm/2016/01/pdf/fm1601.pdf, Table A23, page 97.

[97] Based on the net present value data from the International Monetary Fund, *Fiscal Monitor*, April 2016, http://www.imf.org/external/pubs/ft/fm/2016/01/pdf/fm1601.pdf, Tables A23 and A24 on pages 97 and 98.

[98] Andreades, A. M. 1933. *History of Greek Public Finance*. Cambridge, Mass., in Davies, Glyn. 1994. *A History of Money: From Ancient Times to the Present Day*. University of Wales Press, p. 95.

[99] See, for example, Graeber, David. 2011. *Debt: The First 5,000 Years*, Melville House Publishing, p. 230, where we read about on-going debt crises in Athens and Rome. In Homer, Sidney & Sylla, Richard. 2005. *A History of Interest Rates* (fourth edition). John Wiley & Sons, Inc., we find five thousand years of interest rates, with spikes in rates coinciding with unstable periods. We read that the creditworthiness of most Greek states was not good (p. 37). More recent debt crises have been chronicled in *This Time Is Different: Eight Centuries of Financial Folly* (2011) by Carmen M. Reinhart & Kenneth S. Rogoff, Princeton University Press.

[100] Long-term data from a wide range of countries shows the growth in government taxation, expenditure and debt, as a percentage of GDP, as the role of the state has

grown. The federal government budgets of Australia, Switzerland and the United States are today vastly larger as a share of GDP than they were a century ago. The US Congressional Budget Office projection made in June 2015 forecast federal debt to GDP at close to two hundred per cent of GDP by 2090, even though, at that point the nation is likely to have 120 million more people (i.e. more taxpayers) than today.

It is also of interest to look at the policy impact when compulsory voting is introduced in a democracy. A study of the policy impact of compulsory voting in Australia found that, following its introduction at the national level in 1924, it resulted in a higher increase in state pension spending between 1920 and 1930 when compared to twenty other developed countries. (Source: Fowler, Anthony. 2013. "Electoral and Policy Consequences of Voter Turnout: Evidence from Compulsory Voting in Australia." *Quarterly Journal of Political Science* 8(2):159-182, http://papers.ssrn.com/sol3/papers.cfm?abstract_id=1816649). A study that looked at the policy impact of compulsory voting in the Swiss Canton of Vaud, from 1925 to 1948, found that it resulted in an increase in support for the left, as it drew out more voters from lower incomes who had previously tended not to vote. (Source: Bechtel, Michael M. et al. "Does Compulsory Voting Increase Support for Leftist Policy?" 2015, *American Journal of Political Science*, http://onlinelibrary.wiley.com/doi/10.1111/ajps.12224/epdf).

[101] Shah, Anwahr (ed.). 2007. *Participatory Budgeting*. The World Bank. http://siteresources.worldbank.org/PSGLP/Resources/ParticipatoryBudgeting.pdf

[102]

https://www.google.com/maps/d/viewer?ll=6.839971%2C28.205177&spn=170.95 9424%2C24.609375&hl=en&msa=0&z=1&ie=UTF8&mid=1XSWIeYDu8G8Juw UV2KNfQ9K06EU.

[103] OECD http://www.oecd.org and IMF http://www.imf.org/external/index.htm data. The US number was -4.62 per cent and the Swiss number -0.19 per cent.

[104] Based on the net present value data from the International Monetary Fund, *Fiscal Monitor*, April 2016, http://www.imf.org/external/pubs/ft/fm/2016/01/pdf/fm1601.pdf, Table A23 on page 97.

[105] Davies, Glyn. 1994. *A History of Money*. University of Wales Press, p. 107.

[106] Homer, Sidney & Sylla, Richard. 2005. *A History of Interest Rates.* John Wiley & Sons, Inc.

[107] Executive Order 6102 stated that "All persons are hereby required to deliver on or before May 1, 1933, to a Federal Reserve Bank or a branch or agency thereof or to any member bank of the Federal Reserve System all gold coin, gold bullion and gold certificates now owned by them or coming into their ownership on or before April 28, 1933...". The penalty for noncompliance was ten years' imprisonment and a fine of $10,000 (about $180,000 in 2016 money).

[108] "Treasury-Federal Reserve Accord", March 1951, by Jessie Romero, Federal Reserve Bank of Richmond, http://www.federalreservehistory.org/Events/DetailView/30

[109] Abrams, Burton A. "How Richard Nixon Pressured Arthur Burns: Evidence from the Nixon Tapes", *Journal of Economic Perspectives,* Volume 20, Number 4, Fall 2006, pages 177–188. This type of evidence of political pressure on the central bank tends not to play out in the public arena very often. Six years after he had lost the 1992 presidential election, President George H. W. Bush felt comfortable enough to publicly state for the first time that the reason why he had lost that election was because of Alan Greenspan, Chairman of the US Federal Reserve. In a television interview, he said: "I reappointed him, and he disappointed me in the way that they begrudgingly lowered the rates. I think that if the interest rates had been lowered more dramatically that I would have been re-elected president." Source: Television interview of President George H. W. Bush by David Frost (1998).

Former French President Sarkozy criticized the head of the European Central Bank in 2007 for not cutting rates. He accused the central bank of making life difficult for entrepreneurs. He also wanted a cheaper euro. (Source: "Jean-Claude Trichet rejette les critiques de Nicolas Sarkozy sur la BCE", 16 September 2007, *Le Monde,*
 http://www.lemonde.fr/societe/article/2007/09/15/jean-claude-trichet-repond-a-nicolas-sarkozy_955752_3224.html).

And then we have the case of the president of Turkey teaching the central bank in public to do the exact opposite of what the text books say: If you lower interest rates, you get lower inflation, he told an audience of small business owners. Why didn't the central bank get it? (Source: Meric, Ali Berat and Ant, Onur, "Erdogan

Renews Assault on Turkish Central Bank's Monetary Policy", 4 February 2015, Bloomberg, https://www.bloomberg.com/news/articles/2015-02-04/erdogan-you-can-t-decide-interest-rates-according-to-inflation).

Against the background of how presidents in America and Europe have pressured their central banks to keep rates low, we can only imagine what pearls of monetary policy wisdom were shared over tea by the president of Zimbabwe and the governor of his central bank. The central bank's "overnight accommodation rate" reached 40,000 per cent in November 2008. That was a very accommodating rate indeed, considering that inflation was then around 80 billion per cent. (Source: Monetary Policy Statement, January 2009, Reserve Bank of Zimbabwe, http://rbz.co.zw/assets/mpsjan2009.pdf).

[110] Saad, Lydia. 27 July 2009, "NASA ratings remain high, while Federal Reserve has lost ground", http://www.gallup.com/poll/121886/cdc-tops-agency-ratings-federal-reserve-board-lowest.aspx

[111] McMahon, Madeline. 16 October 2015. "Trump: Janet Yellen Keeping Interest Rates Low as Political Favor to Obama", *Bloomberg*, http://www.bloomberg.com/politics/articles/2015-10-16/trump-speaks-in-bloomberg-tv-interview-on-janet-yellen-interest-rates

[112] European Commission, Eurobarometer of November 2015, http://ec.europa.eu/public_opinion/index_en.htm

[113] Cullen, Angela & Black, Jeff. "ECB's Celebration of Its New $1.4 Billion Tower Is Spoiled by Protesters", 18 March 2015, *Bloomberg*, http://www.bloomberg.com/news/articles/2015-03-18/ecb-besieged-by-protests-as-draghi-celebrates-1-4-billion-tower

[114] Bernanke, Ben S. "Remarks by Governor Ben S. Bernanke At the Conference to Honor Milton Friedman, University of Chicago, Chicago, Illinois, November 8, 2002, On Milton Friedman's Ninetieth Birthday", http://www.federalreserve.gov/boarddocs/speeches/2002/20021108/default.htm

[115] Sources: For the period 1700 to 1949, constructed from data points for population and GDP estimates in Madison, Angus, 2003, "The World Economy: historical statistics", OECD. For the period 1950 to 2015, GDP and population data from the IMF, the UN population database and country data.

[116] Article 13 of "The Liberties of the Massachusets Collonie in New England", 1641.

[117] "A Century of Trends in Adult Human Height," eLife 2016;5:e13410, July 26, 2016, https://elifesciences.org/content/5/e13410

[118] Freund, Caroline. 2016. "Rich People Poor Countries: The Rise of Emerging-Market Tycoons and their Mega Firms", Peter G. Peterson Institute for International Economics, http://www.piie.com

[119] World Economic Forum. 2016. *The Global Gender Gap Index, 2015*. "Table C14: Years with female head of state." http://reports.weforum.org/global-gender-gap-report-2015/appendix-c/

[120] International Parliamentary Union. "Women in national parliaments", as of 1 February 2016, http://www.ipu.org/wmn-e/classif.htm

[121] "Country Status on the Death Penalty", as of 30 June 2015, http://www.handsoffcain.info/

[122] The International Property Rights Index 2015, http://internationalpropertyrightsindex.org

[123] Heritage Foundation. "2016 Index of Economic Freedom", http://www.heritage.org/index/ranking

[124] Rubin, Richard. "Cash Abroad Rises $206 Billion as Apple to IBM Avoid Tax", 12 March 2014, *Bloomberg,* http://www.bloomberg.com/news/articles/2014-03-12/cash-abroad-rises-206-billion-as-apple-to-ibm-avoid-tax

[125] Other examples of this type of "big country" behaviour include the sweeping ban on the import of food from the US, Canada, the European Union, Norway and Australia announced by Russia in August 2014. A small country would never have dreamt of doing such a thing, but when your country has eleven time zones, you don't think like a small country, and you certainly don't think about competitiveness. Another example is the hike in the top tax rate in France from forty-five per cent to seventy-five per cent in 2013. When the French actor Gerard Depardieu subsequently renounced his citizenship and left the country, the French Prime Minister, Jean-Marc Ayrault, called Depardieu's decision "unpatriotic".

Only twelve thousand households would have been affected by this tax hike, and France is a big country, after all, and has many households – competitiveness is for the little ones, not for France.

[126] "America's Berlin Wall", 12 June 2008, *The Economist*, http://www.economist.com/node/11554721

[127] Illegal Immigration Reform and Immigrant Responsibility Act of 1996

[128] *Federal Register*, "Quarterly Publication of Individuals, Who Have Chosen To Expatriate, as Required by Section 6039G", www.gpo.gov

[129] Estimating Net International Migration for 2010 Demographic Analysis: An Overview of Methods and Results, Population Division Working Paper No. 97, US Census Bureau, February 2013, p. 8, http://www.census.gov/population/www/documentation/twps0097/twps0097.pdf

[130] "President Obama Praises New Inversion Rules", Dow Jones & Company, Inc., 5 April 2016, http://www.nasdaq.com/article/president-obama-praises-new-inversion-rules-20160405-00837

[131] Plato, *The Republic* (translated by Benjamin Jowett), Book VIII.

[132] See, for example, http://p2pfoundation.net/Liquid_Democracy; Ford, Bryan. 2002. "Delegative Democracy", http://www.brynosaurus.com/deleg/deleg.pdf; Rodriguez, Marko A. et al., 2007, "Smartocracy: Social Networks for Collective Decision-Making", http://public.lanl.gov/jhw/Jen/Publications_files/Smarto-Share.pdf; Boldi, Paolo et al. "Voting in Social Networks", http://www-kdd.isti.cnr.it/~bonchi/votingSN.pdf; https://groups.yahoo.com/neo/groups/sd-2/info; Ito, Joichi, 2003. "Emergent Democracy", http://joi.ito.com/joiwiki/EmergentDemocracyPaper. See also, Chalmers, Patrick, "The people trying to save democracy from itself", in *The Guardian*, https://www.theguardian.com/world/2016/jul/02/democracy-tarnished-brand-desperate-need-reinvention

[133] See the reference in Chapter 4 to falling membership of political parties, globally, and to declining levels of individual identification with a single party. Moreover, the disintermediation of the legislative process is underway in several countries via different routes: a minimalist option that allows citizens to petition their parliament electronically and a maximalist option that allows the people to

write the entire legislative text via an online process. Google reportedly contributed to funding a crowdsourcing project for France's legislature that resulted in a 2015 bill integrating ninety external contributions. In a similar process in Taiwan, the public has been able to influence several pieces of legislation, from company law, alcohol sales and Airbnb-type activities. In Brazil, around thirty per cent of the final text for one piece of legislation is reported to have come from the public via crowdsourcing. Source: Simon, Julie et al. February 2017, *Digital Democracy*, http://www.nesta.org.uk/sites/default/files/digital_democracy.pdf, p. 24 for the reference to France, p. 29 for the reference about Taiwan, and p. 20 for the reference about Brazil.

[134] Cachelin, Joël Luc. 2016. *Update! Warum die digitale Gesellschaft ein neues Betriebssystem braucht.* Stämpfli.

[135] Van Reybrouck, David. 2013 (English translation: 2016 by Liz Waters). *Against Elections: The Case for Democracy.* The Bodley Head.

[136] World Values Survey, 2012.

[137] European Commission, Eurobarometer of November 2015, http://ec.europa.eu/public_opinion/index_en.htm

[138] "Apenas 14% dos brasileiros se dizem satisfeitos com a democracia", IBPOE, 25 April 2016, http://www.ibopeinteligencia.com/noticias-e-pesquisas/apenas-14-dos-brasileiros-se-dizem-satisfeitos-com-a-democracia/

[139] Eurostat. "Average rating of trust by domain, income quintile, household type and degree of urbanization", 2013 data, with last update on 15 March 2016, http://ec.europa.eu/eurostat/web/products-datasets/-/ilc_pw04

[140] United Kingdom Parliament. Act No XI, Declaration of the Powers on the affairs of the Helvetic Confederacy of the 20th March; and Act of Ascension of the Diet of the 27th of May 1815. *Journals of the House of Commons.*

[141] ibid.

[142] Of course, the story is a little more complicated than just a dispute about a bridge. The Germans, in turn, were upset about an article in a Swiss newspaper and the Swiss confiscation of Catholic church property. Source: Inauen Josef. 2008.

Brennpunkt Schweiz: die süddeutschen Staaten Baden, Württemberg und Bayern und die Eidgenossenschaft 1815-1840. Academic Press Fribourg, p. 212.

[143] Mettler, Jon. 17 February 2015. *Berner Zeitung.* http://www.bernerzeitung.ch/schweiz/standard/Der-Terrorismus-forderte-in-der-Schweiz-bislang-60-Tote/story/16380003

[144] "Weniger Risiko-Personen in der Armee", *Schweiz am Sonntag*, 6 March 2016.

[145] The average of 192 countries, based on 2015 data. Sources: Official cabinet websites.

[146] Article 139 (3) of the Swiss federal constitution.

[147] In practice, there is a restriction, namely that the initiative should not address an issue that would cause the country to be in violation of an area of human rights law from which no country can get an exemption (such as a crime against humanity).

[148] Article 141 of the Swiss federal constitution.

[149] With regard to human rights, the Swiss have agreed to be subjected to the jurisdiction of an external court – the European Court for Human Rights, based in Strasbourg, France. A negative ruling by that court could require changes in Swiss legislation or cause the Swiss supreme court to provide relief or compensation in that specific case.

[150] Even though Britain did not have a written constitution.

[151] Raphael, Ray. 2012. *Mr. President: How and Why the Founders Created a Chief Executive.* Random House.

[152] "Angenommene und verworfene Abstimmungsvorlagen, nach Typ", 1848-Februar 2016, Bundesamt für Statistik, http://www.bfs.admin.ch/bfs/portal/de/index/themen/17/03/blank/key/eidg__volksi nitiativen.html

[153] "Across the Aisle with Senators Trent Lott and Tom Daschle on 'Crisis Point', Discussion at the Edward M. Kennedy Institute", 21 January 2016, https://www.emkinstitute.org/explore-the-institute/public-events-programs/public/ata2016lottdaschle

[154] http://www.nytimes.com/2004/07/14/us/virginia-lawmakers-trudge-back-to-scene-to-repair-error.html?pagewanted=1&_r=0

[155] Based on data from Scotusblog for the period from 2008 to 2015, http://www.scotusblog.com/wp-content/uploads/2016/06/SB_unanimity_OT15.pdf

[156] Cosgrove-Mather, Bootie, 23 January 2003, "Poll: Talk First, Fight Later", http://www.cbsnews.com/news/poll-talk-first-fight-later/15

[157] European Commission. Survey Question: "Should immigration policy be made by the UK government or jointly with the EU?" Percentage of British residents saying it should be made by the UK government: 66% in October 1999, 65% in October 2001 and 67% in October 2003, http://ec.europa.eu/COMMFrontOffice/publicopinion/index.cfm/Chart/getChart/themeKy/10/groupKy/253

[158] See, for example, Bowler, Shaun et al. 2003. "Popular Attitudes towards Direct Democracy", http://faculty.wwu.edu/donovat/bdkapsa03.pdf

[159] Thornton, John L., "Long Time Coming: The Prospects for Democracy in China", *Foreign Affairs*, January / February 2008.

Index

Lightning Source UK Ltd.
Milton Keynes UK
UKOW05f1145270617
304177UK00002B/364/P